A World Without Privacy

Recent revelations about America's National Security Agency offer a stark reminder of the challenges posed by the rise of the digital age for American law. These challenges refigure the meaning of autonomy and the meaning of the word "social" in an age of new modalities of surveillance and social interaction, as well as new reproductive technologies and the biotechnology revolution. Each of these developments seems to portend a world without privacy, or at least a world in which the meaning of privacy is radically transformed, both as a legal idea and a lived reality. Each requires us to rethink the role that law can and should play in responding to today's threats to privacy.

Can the law keep up with emerging threats to privacy? Can it provide effective protection against new forms of surveillance? This book offers some answers to these questions. It considers several different understandings of privacy and provides examples of legal responses to the threats to privacy associated with new modalities of surveillance, the rise of digital technology, the excesses of the Bush and Obama administrations, and the continuing war on terror.

Austin Sarat is William Nelson Cromwell Professor of Jurisprudence Political Science at Amherst College, where he is also Associate Dean of the Faculty, and Justice Hugo

L. Black Senior Faculty Scholar at the University of Alabama School of Law. He is the author or editor of numerous books, including *Gruesome Spectacles: Botched Executions and America's Death Penalty* (with Katherine Blumstein, Aubrey Jones, Heather Richard, and Madeline Sprung-Keyser, 2014); *Re-imagining* To Kill a Mockingbird: *Family, Community, and the Possibility of Equal Justice under Law* (2013); *Legal Responses to Religious Practices in the United States: Accommodation and its Limits* (2012); and *Civility, Legality, and the Limits of Justice* (2014). Sarat is the editor of the journals *Law, Culture and the Humanities*, and *Studies in Law, Politics and Society*. His book *When Government Breaks the Law: Prosecuting the Bush Administration* was named one of the best books of 2010 by the *Huffington Post*.

A World Without Privacy

What Law Can
and Should Do?

Edited by

AUSTIN SARAT

Amherst College

CAMBRIDGE
UNIVERSITY PRESS

CAMBRIDGE
UNIVERSITY PRESS

32 Avenue of the Americas, New York, NY 10013-2473, USA

Cambridge University Press is part of the University of Cambridge.

It furthers the University's mission by disseminating knowledge in the pursuit of education, learning, and research at the highest international levels of excellence.

www.cambridge.org
Information on this title: www.cambridge.org/9781107081215

© Austin Sarat 2015

First published 2015

A catalog record for this publication is available from the British Library.

Library of Congress Cataloging in Publication Data
A world without privacy : what law can and should do? / edited
by Austin Sarat.
  pages cm
ISBN 978-1-107-08121-5 (hardback)
1. Privacy, Right of – United States.   2. Surveillance detection – United
States.   I. Sarat, Austin, editor.
KF1262.W67   2014
342.7308′58–dc23

                                                                    2014023803

ISBN 978-1-107-08121-5 Hardback

Contents

Contents

Contributors

Lisa M. Austin is Associate Professor of Law at the University of Toronto Faculty of Law

Kevin Haggerty is Professor Criminology and Sociology at the University of Alberta

Ronald Krotoszynski is John S. Stone Chairholder of Law and Director of Faculty Research at the School of Law at the University of Alabama

Neil Richards is Professor of Law at Washington University School of Law

Rebecca L. Tushnet is Professor of Law at Georgetown School of Law

Austin Sarat is Associate Dean of the Faculty and William Nelson Cromwell Professor of Jurisprudence & Political Science at Amherst College and Justice Hugo L. Black Visiting Senior Scholar at the School of Law at the University of Alabama

Whither Privacy? An Introduction

Austin Sarat

Recent revelations about the US National Security Agency offer a stark reminder of the challenges posed for US law by the rise of the digital age.[1] These challenges refigure the meaning of autonomy and the social in the face of new modalities of surveillance. We live in an age of new modalities of social interaction as well as new reproductive technologies and the biotechnology revolution. Each of these things seems to portend a world without privacy, or at least a world in which the meaning of privacy is radically transformed both as a legal idea and a lived reality. Each requires us to rethink

---

[1] See, for example, "NSA Surveillance Exposed," *CBS News*, available at http://www.cbsnews.com/feature/nsa-surveillance-exposed (accessed January 20, 2014).

the role that law can and should play in responding to today's threats to privacy.[2]

These concerns are, of course, not unique to the early twenty-first century. More than a hundred years ago, Samuel Warren and Louis Brandeis warned of emerging threats to individual liberty associated with new business methods and technologies.[3] "Instantaneous photographs and newspaper enterprise," they said, "have invaded the sacred precincts of private and domestic life; and numerous mechanical devices threaten to make good the prediction that 'what is whispered in the closet shall be proclaimed from the house-tops.'"[4] Warren and Brandeis worried, in particular, about the press "overstepping in every direction the obvious bounds of propriety and of decency." "Gossip," they observed, "is no longer the resource of the idle and of the vicious, but has become a trade, which is pursued with industry as well as effrontery. To satisfy a prurient taste the

---

[2] Much of what follows is taken from Austin Sarat, Lawrence Douglas, & Martha Umphrey, "Change and Continuity: Privacy and Its Prospects in the 21st Century," in *Imaging New Legalities: Privacy and Its Possibilities in the 21st Century*, eds. Austin Sarat, Lawrence Douglas, & Martha Umphrey (Stanford, Ca: Stanford University Press, 2012).

[3] Samuel Warren & Louis Brandeis, "The Right to Privacy," *Harvard Law Review* 4 (1890), 193. For another formulation of this right see Guy Thompson, "The Right of Privacy as Recognized and Protected at Law and Equity," *Central Law Journal* 47 (1898), 148. See also Patricia Ann Meyer Spacks, *Privacy: Concealing the Eighteenth-Century Self* (Chicago: University of Chicago Press, 2003).

[4] *Ibid.*, 195.

details of sexual relations are spread in the columns of the daily papers. To occupy the indolent, column upon column is filled with idle gossip, which can only be procured by intrusion upon the domestic circle."[5]

Against this background, Warren and Brandeis identified a right to privacy implicit in the Anglo-American common law that afforded individuals "full protection in person and property."[6] They set out to "define anew the exact nature and extent of such protection"; that is, to adjust the meaning of the right to privacy to meet the demands of a rapidly changing society.[7] They called for explicit legal recognition of the "right to be let alone."[8] As they saw it, this right is itself part of a more "general right to the immunity of person."[9] It is, in their words, "the right to one's personality."[10]

---

[5] *Ibid.*, 196.

[6] *Ibid.*, 198.

[7] *Ibid.* See also Francis Bohlen, "Fifty Years of Torts," *Harvard Law Review* 50 (1936), 731.

[8] *Ibid.*, 205. For an extended discussion of this formulation see Morris Ernst and Alan Schwartz, *Privacy: The Right To Be Let Alone* (New York: Macmillan), 1962.

[9] *Ibid.* For a different view see Rufus Lisle, "The Right of Privacy (A Contra View)," *Kentucky Law Journal* 19 (1930), 137.

[10] *Ibid.* Writing in 1968, as new technologies began to threaten increasingly invasive government intrusion into the traditional private sphere, Charles Fried identified "a new sense of urgency in the defense of privacy." See Charles Fried, "Privacy," *Yale Law Journal* 77 (1968), 475. In attempting to discover the theoretical foundations of the "right to privacy," he found that privacy allows us to develop the relationships that make us human. According to Fried, the protection

Warren and Brandeis' justifiably famous article offers but one important example of the challenges that threats to privacy pose to law. They carefully reworked the materials of the common law to fashion a new legal concept. Confronting changes in society, they set out to identify new legal responses to changed circumstances. The question for our time is whether we can identify similar responses in light of contemporary challenges. The work collected here offers examples of the way scholars are responding to those challenges. It ranges from full-throated defenses of privacy and optimistic offerings of new legal devices to protect it, to deep pessimism and doubt that the law can keep up with erosions in the lived reality of privacy.

While the US Constitution makes no explicit reference to a "right to privacy," by the late twentieth century that right was as venerated as any other right and arguably is as inseparable from liberty as any democratic ideal.[11] At the

of individual autonomy is the "necessary context for relationships which we would hardly be human if we had to do without – the relationships of love, friendship, and trust." *Ibid.*, 477. He argues that the principles of "love, friendship, and trust" are at "the heart of our notion of ourselves as persons among persons." *Ibid.*, 478.

[11] The 1987 hearings on the nomination of Robert Bork to be a Justice of the United States Supreme Court provide one piece of evidence of such veneration. Explaining why he could not support Bork, Republican Senator Robert Packwood explained, "I am convinced that Judge Bork feels so strongly opposed to the right of privacy that he will do everything possible to cut and trim, and eliminate if possible, the liberties that the right of privacy protects."

See Linda Greenhouse, "The Bork Hearings: Packwood, Seeing Threat to Privacy, Opposes Bork," *The New York Times*

same time, the late twentieth century gave rise to trenchant questions about the very coherence or desirability of defending privacy.[12] Today, threats to privacy are ubiquitous. They take the form of new modalities of surveillance, new reproductive technologies, the biotechnology revolution, the rise of the digital technology, the excesses of the Bush Administration, and the continuing war on terror.

This book does not seek to provide a comprehensive overview of threats to privacy and rejoinders to them. Instead it considers several different conceptions of privacy and provides examples of challenges to it. In the remainder of this introduction I survey the meanings of privacy in three domains: the first, involving intimacy and intimate relations; the second, implicating criminal procedure through, in particular, the Fourth Amendment; and the third, addressing control of information in the digital age. The first two provide examples of what are taken to be classic invasions of privacy, namely instances when government intrudes in an area claimed to be private. The third has to do with voluntary circulation of information and the question of who gets to control what happens to and with that information.

(September 22, 1987), available at http://www.nytimes.com/1987/09/22/us/the-bork-hearings-packwood-seeing-threat-to-privacy-opposes-bork.html

[12] See, for example, Duncan Kennedy, "The Stages of the Decline of the Public/Private Distinction," *University of Pennsylvania Law Review* 130 (1982), 1349. Also Robert Mnookin, "The Public/Private Dichotomy: Political Disagreement and Academic Repudiation," *University of Pennsylvania Law Review* 130 (1982), 1429.

Intimacy and Privacy

In the realm of intimate relations, the right to privacy was first recognized in the landmark 1965 case of *Griswold v. Connecticut*.[13] In *Griswold*, the US Supreme Court struck down a Connecticut law banning the sale or use of contraceptives to, and by, married couples. The court identified a right to privacy grounded in the "penumbras" and "emanations" of the First, Third, Fourth, Fifth, and Ninth Amendments to the US Constitution and argued that the right to privacy in marriage was older than the Bill of Rights itself.[14] As Justice Douglas put it,

> We deal with a right of privacy older than the Bill of Rights – older than our political parties, older than our school system. Marriage is a coming together for better or for worse, hopefully enduring, and intimate to the degree of being sacred. It is an association that promotes a way of life, not causes; a harmony in living, not political faiths; a bilateral loyalty, not commercial or social projects. Yet it is an association for as noble a purpose as any involved in our prior decisions.[15]

Eisenstadt v. Baird (1972)[16] extended *Griswold*'s privacy protections to unmarried individuals, a shift in logic that provided the doctrinal basis for the court's subsequent decision to

---

[13] *Griswold v. Connecticut*, 381 U.S. 479 (1965).
[14] *Ibid.*, 484.
[15] *Ibid.*, 488.
[16] *Eisenstadt v. Baird*, 405 U.S. 438 (1972).

protect women's reproductive freedom in *Roe v. Wade*[17] and its decision striking down a Texas anti-sodomy statute in *Lawrence v. Texas.*[18] Michael Sandel argues that this doctrinal path is marked by a regrettable change from Douglas' substantive assertions about the value of marriage to what Sandel calls a "voluntarist conception" of privacy grounded in the belief in the "neutral state" and the desirability of an "unencumbered self."[19] The voluntarist conception is associated with the belief that government should remain neutral among different conceptions of the good so that individuals can freely choose how to lead their own lives.[20]

As Sandel sees it, "So close is the connection between privacy rights and the voluntarist conception of the self that commentators frequently assimilate the values of privacy and autonomy."[21] Thus, Jon Mills writes, "Individual privacy is at the core of personal identity and personal freedom."[22] Moreover, in "Supreme Court decisions and dissents alike,

[17] *Roe v. Wade*, 410 U.S. 113 (1973).

[18] *Lawrence v. Texas*, 539 U.S. 558 (2003).

[19] Michael Sandel, *Democracy's Discontent: America in Search of a Public Philosophy* (Cambridge: Harvard University Press, 1998), 91. Andrew Taslitz argues that "to invade privacy is to unsettle our very identity, distorting relationships with others, self-esteem, and self-concept." See Andrew Taslitz, "The Fourth Amendment in the Twenty-First Century: Technology, Privacy, and Human Emotions," *Law and Contemporary Problems* 65 (2002), 129–130.

[20] Sandel, *Democracy's Discontent*, 91.

[21] *Ibid.*, 93.

[22] Jon Mills, *Privacy: The Lost Right* (Oxford, UK: Oxford University Press, 2008), 18.

the justices have often tied privacy rights to voluntarist assumptions."[23]

Others join Sandel in criticizing liberalism's tight linkage of privacy and individual autonomy. Daniel Solove, for example, views privacy as more than the protection of autonomy and selfhood when he writes, "Privacy, then, is not the trumpeting of the individual against society's interests, but the protection of the individual based on society's norms and values."[24] He argues that privacy is "not reducible to a singular essence; it is a plurality of different things that do not share one element in common but that nevertheless bear a resemblance to each other."[25] Still others describe the right of privacy as a flight of judicial fancy, ungrounded in the US Constitution itself.[26]

Feminist critics[27] and scholars such as Rosa Ehrenreich warn against the modern preoccupation with the "language

---

[23] Sandel, *Democracy's Discontent*, 92.

[24] Daniel Solove, "'I've Got Nothing to Hide' and Other Misunderstandings of Privacy," *San Diego Law Review* 44 (2007), 763.

[25] *Ibid.*, 756.

[26] John Hart Ely, "The Wages of Crying Wolf: A Comment on Roe v. Wade," *Yale Law Journal* 82 (1973), 920.

[27] See, for example, Ruth Gavison, "Feminism and the Private/Public Distinction." *Stanford Law Review* 45 (1992), 1. Also Linda McClain, "Inviolability and Privacy: The Castle, the Sanctuary, and the Body," *Yale Journal of Law and Humanities* 7 (1995), 195; Elizabeth Schneider, "The Violence of Privacy," *Connecticut Law Review* 23 (1990–1991), 973; Jeannie Suk, "Is Privacy a Woman?," *Georgetown Law Journal* 97 (2009), 485.

of privacy."[28] Writing about *Roe*, Catharine MacKinnon argues that in its reliance on privacy as the basis for women's reproduction rights, *Roe* "translates the ideology of the private sphere into the individual woman's legal right to privacy as a means of subordinating women's collective needs to the imperatives of male supremacy."[29] For MacKinnon, privacy doctrine masks gender inequality by keeping the state out of the home, contributing to state abdication in a realm that requires intervention.

Like MacKinnon, Ehrenreich suggests that "privacy issues ... might be better described and analyzed as issues of *power*."[30] She writes, "The problem with the concept of 'privacy,' however defined, is that whatever work it does, its problematic overuse can obscure certain issues of power and consequential harm."[31] As Ehrenreich points out, generally "those who have power have the luxury of defining what is and what is not private."[32] The denial of privacy, even in civilized societies, becomes a "mechanism of social control."[33]

---

[28] Rosa Ehrenreich, "Privacy and Power," *Georgetown Law Journal* 89 (2001–2002), 2047.

[29] Catharine MacKinnon, *Feminism Unmodified: Discourses on Life and Law* (Cambridge, MA: Harvard University Press, 1987), 93. For a different view see Laura Stein, "Living With the Risk of Backfire: A Response to the Feminist Critiques of Privacy and Equality," *Minnesota Law Review* 77 (1993), 441 and Julie Inness, *Privacy, Intimacy, and Isolation* (New York: Oxford University Press), 1992.

[30] Ehrenreich, "Privacy and Power," 2054 (original emphasis).

[31] *Ibid.*, 2052.

[32] *Ibid.*

[33] *Ibid.*, 2060.

According to Ehrenreich, modernity demands that we "confront the issues of power that lie at the heart of privacy."[34]

Privacy and the Fourth Amendment

At the start of the twentieth century the Fourth Amendment prohibition of unreasonable searches and seizures was rooted in property rights, and a "search" was understood as a physical trespass.[35] Critics of this approach questioned whether "the Constitution affords no protection against such invasions of individual security,"[36] and warned that the property-based conception of the Fourth Amendment rendered it useless as a protection against "subtler and more far-reaching means of invading privacy."[37]

In 1967, the Supreme Court established a new standard for characterizing a Fourth Amendment "search."[38] Justice Stewart, writing for the majority in *Katz v. United States*, argued that "the Fourth Amendment protects people, not places."[39] The *Katz* decision also established a "reasonable

---

[34] *Ibid.*

[35] See *Olmstead v. United States*, 277 U.S. 438, 473–474 (1928).

[36] *Ibid.*

[37] See, for example, Richard Julie, "High-Tech Surveillance Tools and the Fourth Amendment: Reasonable Expectations of Privacy in the Technological Age," *American Criminal Law Review* 37 (2010), 128–129.

[38] See *Katz v. United States*, 389 U.S. 351 (1967).

[39] *Ibid.*, 353.

expectation of privacy" standard for determining whether a Fourth Amendment violation had occurred.[40]

Some now argue that *Katz* did not really alter the doctrinal basis for determining whether an unconstitutional search has occurred. As Kerr writes, "Although no one theory explains the entire body of Fourth Amendment doctrine, property law provides a surprisingly accurate guide."[41] Other Fourth Amendment scholars reject the language of privacy altogether. For example, Thomas Clancy advocates what he calls a "security" approach to the Fourth Amendment and argues

---

[40] *Ibid.* As Justice Harlan put it in his concurring opinion, "As the Court's opinion states, 'the Fourth Amendment protects people, not places.' The question, however, is what protection it affords to those people. Generally, as here, the answer to that question requires reference to a 'place.' My understanding of the rule that has emerged from prior decisions is that there is a twofold requirement, first that a person have exhibited an actual (subjective) expectation of privacy and, second, that the expectation be one that society is prepared to recognize as 'reasonable.'"

As Nissenbaum points out, "various aspects of privacy are, in fact, defended against government action through several of the amendments, including the First (speech, religion, and association), Third (quartering soldiers), Fourth (search and seizure), Fifth (self-incrimination), Ninth (general liberties), and even the Fourteenth (personal liberty versus state action) Amendments." Still, the Fourth Amendment protection against unreasonable search and seizure remains the strongest protection of privacy. See Helen Nissenbaum, "Privacy as Contextual Integrity," *Washington Law Review* 79 (2004), 119.

[41] Orin Kerr, "The Fourth Amendment and New Technologies: Constitutional Myths and the Case for Caution," *Michigan Law Review* 102 (2003–2004), 815.

that the Fourth Amendment was intended to protect "security."[42] He defines this right to "security" as the right to "exclude government agents from unreasonably intruding."[43] Similarly, Jeb Rubenfeld believes that the purpose of the Fourth Amendment is to protect the right of the people as a whole to be secure, arguing that the core meaning of the Fourth Amendment has been obscured by the Court's "overemphasis" on the "reasonable expectation of privacy" doctrine.[44]

Today some commentators worry that, whatever its basis, Fourth Amendment protections and privacy more generally are being eroded.[45] According to Jack Balkin, the government aims to obtain any and as much information as possible and, as a result, Fourth Amendment protections often are inadequate. As he puts it, "electronic surveillance is not its only tool."[46] Today, "Governments can also get information out of human bodies."[47] "Bodies are not simply objects of governance," he notes; "they are rich sources of information that governments can mine through a multitude

---

[42] Thomas Clancy, "What Does the Fourth Amendment Protect: Property, Privacy, or Security," *Wake Forest Law Review* 33 (1998), 307.

[43] *Ibid.*, 316.

[44] See Jed Rubenfeld, "The End of Privacy," *Stanford Law Review* 61 (2008), 101.

[45] For one example see David Lyon, *Surveillance After September 11* (New York: Polity, 2003).

[46] Jack Balkin, "The Constitution in the National Surveillance State." *Minnesota Law Review* 93 (2008–2009), 1.

[47] *Ibid.*

of different technologies and techniques."[48] Genetic information is "particularly sensitive because it reveals unique and immutable attributes" that are not only personal, but shared between family members and across generations.[49]

Writing about the impact of 9/11, Jeffrey Rosen observes that "Before September 11th, the idea that Americans would voluntarily agree to live their lives under the gaze of a network of biometric surveillance cameras, peering at them in government buildings, shopping malls, subways and stadiums, would have seemed unthinkable, a dystopian fantasy of a society that had surrendered privacy and anonymity."[50]

---

[48] *Ibid.*, 6.

[49] See Joanne & Janlori Goldman. "Genetics and Privacy." *American Journal of Law and Medicine* 28 (2002), 285.

[50] See Jeffrey Rosen, "A Watchful State," *New York Times Magazine* (October 7, 2001). See also Rebecca Copeland, "War on Terrorism or War on Constitutional Rights – Blurring the Lines of Intelligence Gathering in Post-September 11 America," *Texas Tech Law Review* 35 (2004), 1 and Sonia Katyal, "The New Surveillance," *Case Western Reserve Law Review* 54 (2003), 238.

See also *United States v. United States District Court* 407 U.S. 297 (1972) (commonly referred to as the *Keith* decision). There the Supreme Court announced what has become the general test for determining whether a foreign intelligence surveillance, or national security, exception should be taken from the Fourth Amendment. The case centered on the question of whether the president should have the power to authorize electronic surveillance without prior judicial approval. While the Court concluded that prior warrant procedures involving judicial approval were necessary before the government could constitutionally conduct covert surveillance, the decision invited Congress to create legislation designed to govern such conduct.

One of the most significant components of the surveillance about which Rosen is concerned is data mining, or "the government's ability to obtain and analyze recorded information about its citizens."[51] Daniel Solove describes data mining as "a new technological tool to pinpoint the terrorists

In 1978, Congress responded to the *Keith* decision and, in part, the Watergate scandal with the Foreign Intelligence Surveillance Act (FISA). FISA was enacted to regulate the use of electronic surveillance within the United States and to prevent terrorism within US borders. FISA also established the Foreign Intelligence Surveillance Court (FISC) to hear applications for electronic surveillance and to provide a check on the power of the executive.

The USA PATRIOT Act was signed into law on October 26, 2001 and modified FISA. The Patriot Act widens the circumstances under which FISA surveillance orders may be granted. The Act does not require that foreign intelligence be the "primacy purpose" of FISA surveillance; instead, the surveillance of foreign powers is allowed if intelligence gathering is only a "significant purpose" of the operations. The Act also redefines the types of surveillance that may be performed in accordance with FISA, meaning that the new act allows for the covert surveillance of email and internet communications. Furthermore, the amount of time foreign intelligence surveillance orders are valid for was expanded under the Patriot Act.

[51] Daniel Solove, "Data Mining and the Security-Liberty Debate," *University of Chicago Law Review* 75 (2008), 343. Solove writes, "Data mining involves creating profiles by collecting and combining personal data and analyzing it for particular patterns of behavior deemed to be suspicious." Jon Mills similarly defines data mining ("transaction surveillance") as involving "the analysis of enormous sums of information – bank records, credit-card activities, phone records, real-estate records, tax returns, travel itineraries and more." See Mills, *Privacy: The Lost Right*, 68.

Much remains to be discovered about the potential uses and abuses of data mining. As Richard Posner notes, "Mining the vast

burrowed in among us."[52] In the past, law enforcement largely had been investigative and reactive. Today the focus is increasingly on prevention. As a result, government and

amount of personal information stored in public and private computer databases is a critical weapon against modern terrorism." Richard Posner, *Not a Suicide Pact: The Constitution in a Time of National Emergency* (New York: Oxford University Press, 2006), 108. In contrast, Solove argues that the efficacy of data mining as a security measure has yet to be fully tested. Solove, "Data Mining and the Security-Liberty Debate." Slobogin makes an even stronger claim when he writes, "What little we know suggests the government's event-driven antiterrorist data mining efforts have been singularly unsuccessful." Christopher Slobogin, "Government Data Mining and the Fourth Amendment," *University of Chicago Law Review* 75 (2008), 324.

[52] See Christopher Slobogin, *Privacy at Risk: The New Government Surveillance and the Fourth Amendment* (Chicago: University of Chicago Press, 2007). Although both Congress and the Supreme Court have regulated electronic surveillance since the emergence of telegraphing technologies in the mid-nineteenth century, in the modern period surveillance law has been driven by primarily statutory rather than constitutional protections. The first significant modern privacy legislation came in response to the *Katz* decision in 1968 with the enactment of the Omnibus and Safe Streets Act ("Title III"). Under the Omnibus Act statutory regime the privacy of both personal and business communications was protected – albeit to a relatively limited degree. Title III constitutes the foundation of foreign electronic surveillance law in the United States. In 1986, Congress passed the Electronic Communications Privacy Act (ECPA). This act updated the requirements of Title III by addressing newer communications technologies such as mobile telephones and email. Both Title III and ECPA requirements apply principally to the monitoring of verbal communications and of electronic and wire communications.

businesses are increasingly partners in surveillance, data mining, and information analysis. Technology allows them to deploy modern "panopticism" as a form of "subtle coercion" against which the Fourth Amendment may be no longer an adequate safeguard.[53]

Digital Technologies and the Erosion of the Public–Private Distinction

The internet and digital technology pose yet other and perhaps more fundamental threats to privacy. Traditionally people worried about public invasions of the private domain, but social networking sites now invite the disclosure of information that previously would have been regarded as private. In the digital age new communities are established and new identities formed, and the threat of intrusion into the private domain no longer primarily or exclusively originates with the state.[54]

Current privacy threats involving the internet are, at least in part, the result of individuals willingly exposing their private lives to millions. "In the digital world of online social networks," Samantha Millier writes, "users have grown accustomed to the free flow of information and expansive

---

[53] Julie Cohen, "Privacy, Visibility, Transparency, and Exposure," *University of Chicago Law Review* 75 (2008), 181.

[54] Samantha Millier, "The Facebook Frontier: Responding to the Changing Face of Privacy on the Internet," *Kentucky Law Journal* 97 (2008–2009), 541.

opportunities for self-expression."[55] As Gelman puts it, "digital dossiers ... are not dossiers compiled by covert spies skulking in dark corners with penlight cameras, nor by government agents scouring the data files held by bid data aggregators." They are autobiographic. In turn, she asks, "Why do people post content on a medium available to the whole world when that content is not intended for the whole world?"[56]

For Gelman, the answer lies in "blurry social networks."[57] In her view, Americans are not exhibitionist, just confused.[58] Internet users often are not entirely sure who has access to their personal information, photos, and videos.[59] "Given the choice," she notes, "of the binary options the internet currently offers – making information available to the world, or password-protecting it for a perfectly defined set – internet posters are choosing the former."[60] People mistakenly believe that what they post will be accessed only by the people for whom they intended it. Moreover, the information individuals post online is rarely limited to identifying information about themselves. The internet has effectively "changed who makes decisions regarding what private

---

[55] Lauren Gelman, "Privacy, Free Speech, and 'Blurry-Edged' Social Networks," *B.C. Law Review* 50 (2009), 1316.

[56] *Ibid.*, 1318.

[57] *Ibid.*

[58] Millier writes, "Many users fail to realize the import of their decisions to pose for a picture or post personal information on their online profiles." See Millier, "The Facebook Frontier ...," 548.

[59] Gelman, "Privacy, Free Speech, and 'Blurry-Edged' Social Networks," 1317–1318.

[60] *Ibid.*, 1319.

information to make public and to which audience to publish it."[61] At the same time, new technology "creates an illusion of privacy and control that users can fall victim to."[62]

The digital age also brings to the fore a tension between privacy protection and market efficiency. As Richard Warner notes, "In general, market economies depend on a flow of information."[63] Wagner argues that technology has greatly improved efficiency, creating the possibility of targeted advertising that, in his view, benefits both businesses and customers.[64] In addition, Peter Swire observes that, despite "the reaction that it is somehow 'creepy' to have everything we browse go into giant databases,"[65] individuals benefit from personalization that such developments allow and companies "get their messages out to the most relevant customers."[66]

Yet even those who see benefits to these new understandings of public and private worry about the dangers posed by

---

[61] *Ibid.*

[62] See Richard Warner, "Surveillance and the Self: Privacy, Identity, and Technology," *DePaul Law Review* 54 (2004–2005), 847. Also Kent Walker, "The Costs of Privacy," *Harvard Journal of Law and Public Policy* 25 (2001), 87.

[63] Warner, "Surveillance and the Self . . .," 847.

[64] Peter Swire, "Peeping," *Berkeley Technology Law Journal* 24 (2009), 1167.

[65] *Ibid.*, 1196.

[66] Warner concedes that data aggregation through which targeted advertising is accomplished "is perhaps the most serious technology-created threat to privacy." He argues that, "If we are to retain our freedom, we need to regain the control that technology has taken from us." Warner, "Surveillance and the Self . . .," 851.

the new technologies. Targeted advertising is accomplished largely by way of data aggregation.[67] When consumers divulge relatively limited pieces of information, it is nearly impossible for them to predict the ways in which that information will be used in the future. "[F]ar from giving us a new sense of control over the face we present to the world," Jeffrey Rosen notes, "the Internet is shackling us to everything that we have ever said, or that anyone has said about us, making the possibility of digital self-reinvention seem like an ideal from a distant era."[68]

Many believe that the law has failed to keep up with the realities of life in the digital world.[69] As Millier puts it, "People's expectations of privacy are transforming, and as social networks such as Facebook scramble to react to these changes, privacy law in the United States has been at a relative standstill."[70] To take but one recent example, in *Moreno v. Hanford Sentinel, Inc.*, the California Court of Appeals dealt with the question of "whether publishing information on a public network available to the world could be

---

[67] Jeffrey Rosen, "The Web Means the End of Forgetting," *New York Times Sunday Magazine* (July 25, 2010), available at http://www.nytimes.com/2010/07/25/magazine/25privacy-t2.html?_r=1&ref=magazine&pagewanted=all

[68] *Ibid.* See also Gelman, "Privacy, Free Speech, and 'Blurry-Edged' Social Networks," 1329.

[69] Millier, "The Facebook Frontier . . .," 543.

[70] *Moreno v. Hanford Sentinel, Inc.*, Court of Appeal of the State of California, FO54138 (2009), available at http://www.courtinfo.ca.gov/opinions/archive/F054138.PDF

considered private if the intent was to reach only a limited audience."[71] Unsurprisingly, the court found that an individual who published information on the internet could not have a reasonable expectation that it would remain private.[72] As a result, some call for new forms of public regulation that they

---

[71] *Ibid.*

[72] See Gelman, "Privacy, Free Speech, and 'Blurry-Edged' Social Networks," 1329. While some view social networking sites as the solution to the privacy dilemma in that they allow some selection in what personal information users disclose, Gelman disagrees. First, social networking sites cut themselves off from the rest of the internet; users "must first become identifiable members of a social network, and then rely on that network to innovate and protect all of the personal information that they collect." Gelman emphasizes the imperfections of privacy policies. Besides, many users do not even understand (or attempt to understand) how privacy controls work. Second, the purpose of these sites is to "capture the economic benefit of users' blurry-edged networks." She writes, "The Facebook platform is built to incent users to disclose more information." Gelman argues, "Herein lies the problem – the design of these sites creates an aura of privacy by suggesting they are for limited disclosure of information to a defined social network of friends." *Ibid.*, 1333.

Gelman proposes a technological solution. She stresses the fact that internet users are left without a means to communicate their privacy preferences or limit third-party uses of personal content online. Therefore, she argues, "One option would be a tool for users to express and exercise privacy preferences over uploaded content." *Ibid.*, 1338. According to Gelman, "Social norms in online communities, as well as existing principles of law, promoted neighborly respect for expressed privacy preferences." *Ibid.* She feels that such a tool might finally allow courts to provide legal privacy protection to the users of social networking sites.

Millier proposes a second technological solution to privacy issues with social networking sites in the form of what she calls "self-help"

hope "can prevent the invasions of privacy resulting from the aggregation of information that, bit by individual bit, poses no privacy threat."[73]

Can law keep up with emerging threats to privacy? Can it provide effective protection against new forms of surveillance? *A World Without Privacy: What Can and Should Law Do?* offers some answers to these questions. The chapters which follow consider several different understandings of privacy and provide examples of legal responses to the threats to privacy associated with new modalities of surveillance, the rise of the digital technology, the excesses of the Bush and Obama Administrations, and the continuing war on terror.

In the first chapter, Neil Richards addresses four common arguments in the privacy debate – privacy is dead, (young) people don't care about privacy, people with nothing

or "self-regulation" technology. She sees potential in the uses of facial recognition software online and writes, "Instead of utilizing such software to create privacy violations, sites like Facebook could be required to offer it to users as a means to notify users when pictures (tagged or untagged) of themselves are uploaded onto the site." Millier, "The Facebook Frontier ...," 551. In this way, users would at least be given the opportunity to protect against the unwanted dissemination of personal photographs. At this point, technology offers only partial solutions to the problems it creates. Although Gelman and Millier seek solutions outside the law, both authors also insist that changes need to be made to privacy law in the United States.

[73] For example, Cohen, "Privacy, Visibility, Transparency, and Exposure."

to hide have nothing to fear, and privacy is bad for business. He believes that each is a "myth" and that they are either "plainly false or deeply misleading." Richards "hopes to clear away some of the confusion surrounding the way we talk about privacy in the digital age" and provide the grounding for constructive debates on how we want to govern our personal information in this information age. These myths derail the debate about privacy which portrays it as outdated or impossible, thereby laying the groundwork for a digital revolution with no rules. Such a response would disempower all but the most powerful among us. Richards argues for an understanding of privacy as "the rules we have in our society for managing the collection, use, and disclosure of personal information."

If we think about privacy as the scope of information we can keep completely secret or unknown, then that kind of privacy is certainly diminishing, but it is in no way "dead." Richards argues that we are living through an information revolution, and the collection, use, and analysis of many kinds of personal data is inevitable. Certain kinds of privacy may fade or become obsolete, but this is natural, because privacy is the product of social norms, and social norms change over time. Yet legal and social rules that govern how information about us is obtained and used (broadly defined) are always necessary, and the information revolution is increasing the importance of these rules rather than decreasing them.

Richards identifies a "privacy paradox": the idea that people indicate a concern about privacy in general, but then act in ways that might seem contradictory; for example, by selling their personal information very cheaply in practice. However, it is also true that "consumers are bewildered and concerned by the difficulties of managing their privacy in practice ... the 'privacy paradox' is thus more likely a symptom of our ineffective system of privacy management than anything else."

Richards argues that "young people," in fact, "care deeply about privacy, but they care about privacy in a different way that reflects their outlook on life." The amount of information that young people share on social media sights may be shocking to adult sensibilities, but adults have found "the youth's" risky behavior shocking for the past fifty years. Furthermore, the context and scope in which this sharing occurs must be taken into account. Online sharing takes place in online forums engineered to maximize data sharing for profit. Social media sites flip the social dynamic from public-through-effort and private-by-default on its head and offer limited, and often confusing privacy options. In addition, the voluntary sharing that takes place is dominantly peer-to-peer: young people often "engage in sophisticated tweaking of the privacy settings" on social networks to protect their information from perceived authority figures.

A more accurate interpretation of the available evidence suggests that people do in fact care about privacy, but they are bewildered by the difficulty of protecting their personal information in a time of rapid technological change and limited options. As Richards states, "When we think about privacy more broadly as the ability of people to participate in how their personal information is collected, processed, and used, it becomes clear that people (and young people) definitely care about this problem."

"If you have nothing to hide, you have nothing to fear." This argument views "privacy" as no more than the ability to hide unpleasant truths from public scrutiny. By framing the question of privacy, Richards claims, around the existence of a proverbial dirty secret it ignores the reasons why privacy matters in three separate ways. First, all of us have something to hide, or at the very least information that we don't want broadcast to the world. Second, this argument is misleading because it treats privacy as an individual, not social value. "Rather than thinking about privacy as merely the individual right to hide bad deeds, we should think more broadly about the kind of society we want to live in."

Finally, "reducing privacy to an individual right to hide dark secrets ignores the power effects of privacy. Information is power it provides the power to blackmail, persuade, and classify." We already recognize the power of individualized information exchange in confidentiality laws, but this understanding must be expanded in the face of modern day data-based analytics that aggregate seemingly trivial bits of personal information to increase the persuasive power of already powerful entities – political machines, corporations, and others.

A final argument holds that "we have a free internet built on personalized advertising, which requires that businesses know about the people surfing the web," so if we halted the free flow of information our digital revolution would grind to a halt. In fact, Richards says, the internet demonstrates that personal information is extremely economically valuable: thousands of companies are willing to *exchange* complex services for personal data. So, from a narrow perspective, requiring businesses to account for privacy would make things more expensive, but "customers share their data with companies under the expectation that it will be treated ethically and responsibly. There is good evidence that consumers share because they think that privacy law is considerably more protective than it really is." Privacy could become a space in which competitive innovation can occur among businesses.

Unless we correct myths about privacy, Richards worries that it will simply evolve in a way that favors the interests of the few over the interests of the many. In a democratic information society, the basic rules for information flow (privacy), he says, should be decided through public deliberation, rather than "technocratic isolation." We must balance the values of privacy, autonomy, security, and profitability, among others.

Chapter 2 by Rebecca Tushnet considers one privacy practice in the digital age and offers a "feminist account of some of the affordances of pseudonymity." Though she recognizes the capacity of anonymity to preserve "private (generally white and male) power over others," she argues that requiring "real names" in internet discourse threatens more than abstract notions of free speech but also the "everyday project of the creation of the self." She argues that pseudonymity, or the "practice of maintaining separate, persistent identities, is not inherently disreputable or suspect," but actually enables the creation of "rich communities and interactive works of art."

To illustrate her argument, she offers two examples, encapsulated in the title of her chapter, that highlight the way the stakes in anonymity and pseudonymity differ by gender. The Yes Men, pranksters who impersonate powerful figures for political ends, skirt the boundaries of trademark laws but courts have ruled that their actions are protected by the First Amendment "in the specific instance of nonprofit impersonation designed to highlight and criticize an impersonated organization." *The Women Men Don't See* is an award-winning short story about two women who decide to leave the planet to escape the oppression of misogyny and male dominance. Tushnet contrasts this "opting out" with women on the internet who use pseudonymity as a defensive power allowing them to "opt in" to internet communities without subjecting themselves to discrimination and repression.

Both the Yes Men and the pseudonymous women of the internet are afforded specific benefits by their pseudonymity, and these benefits are "under threat in a pervasively tracked and re-identified world." The Yes Men adopt the language, mannerisms, legal rights, and cultural customs of corporations to engage with them on their own terms. In a 2010 prank, the Yes Men forged a Koch Industries press release stating that Koch would stop funding organizations that deny climate change.

Pseudonymity, Tushnet argues, can be a powerful tool in protecting marginalized groups and creating female-friendly creative spaces. "Many people, particularly those who are extremely secure in their identities (especially those who are white, male, and steadily employed), have little sympathy for pseudonymic participation." Furthermore, Tushnet argues that pseudonyms can play an integral role in driving internet communities because they "are better than legal names for the purpose at hand: expression and representation of the self to a particular community." Pseudonyms leave behind personal ties without sacrificing personality and allow for a creative flowing of marginalized art forms. "Thus, the discourse of threat and risk that understandably begins most defenses of pseudonyms online isn't the whole picture. There's also welcome, comfort, and community to be found in pseudonyms."

Moreover, there is pleasure in assuming a different social identity. Like Richards, Tushnet believes that some people have utterly legitimate things to hide, and that pseudonymity has the productive power to yield creativity and community as individuals craft contextually based names for themselves. "Separated, persistent identities are a way for people to create themselves, and to create new works of art, taking advantage of the power that comes from being unseen or partially seen." Pseudonyms are one example of the positive uses of privacy in a world of increasing transparency.

In the next chapter, Lisa Austin argues that, if we want to revive privacy from its current "death throes," attending to the activities of state authorities is not enough. To properly address the needs of the information age, we need to understand the business model of surveillance and the role of law in enabling both it and the corporate–state nexus. Austin argues that current paradigms for preserving privacy that revolve around informational self-determination and conceptions of consent are inadequate. She offers an alternative schema based on informational power dynamics.

Consent-based models of privacy protection seek to empower "individuals to have control over the collection, use, and disclosure of their personal information." In fact, "comprehensive consent-based private-sector privacy legislation" may actually serve to enable an increasing infrastructure of surveillance. With regard to internet surveillance, social media, lawful access, and the information practices associated with analyzing metadata, the consent model operates to undermine privacy and to some extent facilitate surveillance.

Austin further rejects the tort- and constitutional-law based conceptions of privacy because they focus on regulating "private" information rather than personal information. Echoing Richards, she cautions that they "repeatedly fall back on ideas of privacy that it to intimate confidential or sensitive information," yielding an overly narrow view.

The alternative Austin proposes "is to focus on power." This power-centric approach is comprised of "two components which take two different lessons from ideas about trespass." A "power-over" analysis draws on the power-restraining conception of "the rule of law." "Instead of focusing primarily on questions such as one's reasonable expectation of privacy, it could focus on the surveilling party and questions of power, its possibility of abuse, and legal safeguards. It would place questions of transparency and accountability at the center of the debate rather than as add-ons to the reasonable expectation of privacy analysis." Choice and consent are not the central ideas in this approach; "instead they involve a recognition of the limits of the ideas of individual choice and consent."

A "power-to" analysis draws from the lesson that "trespass liability is not about redressing harms but about protecting the control powers of owners." This connects privacy to the "facilitative role law plays." Drawing on trespass tort law, this approach "reflect[s] the nature of the right of possession as one of exclusive control. Austin argues that if we liberate privacy thinking from its search for privacy harms" we can think about privacy norms as securing our "ability of self-presentation" through audience segregation.

Chapter 4 by Kevin Haggerty aims to "evaluate the entire privacy infrastructure, and asks if the wide array of laws designed to protect privacy, when looked at as a whole, offers realistic hope of insulating us from the powerful forces coalescing to reduce the lived experience of privacy." He argues that privacy has been in decline for over a century and, unlike Richards or Tushnet, he thinks that the current "privacy infrastructure is ill equipped to check this trend." Haggerty defines privacy as "a place (simultaneously spatial, psychological, and informational) where individuals are relatively free from interpersonal or institutional scrutiny." He is interested in privacy as what he calls "a lived reality." Privacy, understood in this way, can be reduced through means that are not classically understood as privacy violations – for example, an extreme exhibitionist who publishes her innermost thoughts online experiences a reduction in the lived reality of privacy through the act of purely voluntary sharing.

Haggerty makes a three-part claim. First, he claims that the privacy infrastructure has not been particularly successful over the long term in curtailing the expansion of surveillance and attendant reductions in the lived reality of privacy. Second, like Austin, he notes that regulations justified as a way to protect privacy can actually serve to expand surveillance. Finally, developments in information capitalism threaten to drastically reconfigure, or even overwhelm, privacy protections over the course of several decades.

Though "there have never been more privacy laws, a richer professional discourse on the topic, or a more extensive and dedicated network of privacy professionals," the unrelenting expansion and intensification of surveillance indicts the privacy infrastructure. Some factors that limit the efficacy of privacy regulations include (1) a judicially based system of privacy redress that favors the very powerful institutional actors that support greater surveillance; (2) a judicial standard of "reasonable privacy expectation" that cyclically justifies increasing levels of surveillance; (3) the necessary constraints that privacy standards place on bureaucratic efficiency, economic competition, or personal security; (4) the often intangible or hypothetical nature of privacy violations justified by comparatively concrete national security concerns; and (5) the fact that courts will only restrict surveillance that infringes on personal rights, thereby green-lighting surveillance practices that fall below that threshold but nevertheless reduce the sphere of personal privacy.

Haggerty asserts that, over the past hundred years, surveillance capacity has expanded and privacy has correspondingly decreased. Furthermore, he says, "we can predict the informational needs of capitalism, combined with the influence of the surveillance industrial complex, will profoundly strain, or perhaps even overwhelm, longstanding privacy protections." For Haggerty, it is the private sector and the birth of "informational capitalism" based on big data analytics, not the state, that presents the greatest threat to privacy. Haggerty asserts that "when longstanding rights impede a new form of capitalism, those rights risk being trounced." The established privacy rights and fair information practices that currently stand in the way of organizational access to and use of certain forms of data are already experiencing this incremental decline.

Furthermore, corporations have identified surveillance as a growth market and are developing, marketing, and advocating for a litany of new surveillance products. "The result has been the emergence of a surveillance industrial complex characterized by intimate relationships between government officials and corporate lobbyists eager to secure lucrative government contracts for their new surveillance devices. This symbiotic relationship is oriented to maximizing profits while expanding the circuits of social control, and in the process reducing the lived reality of privacy." Ultimately, in Haggerty's view, the fact that "we are living through an information revolution" makes the collection, use, and analysis of many kinds of personal data inevitable. This marks, he believes, the death of privacy.

The book concludes with an Afterword and reflections on the previous chapters by Ronald J. Krotoszynski. Taken together, the work collected here illustrates the contingencies and complexities attached to the idea of privacy and the law's efforts to protect it.

1

Four Privacy Myths

Neil M. Richards

A ny discussion about privacy today inevitably confronts a series of common arguments about the futility of privacy in our digital age. "Privacy is dead," we hear, and "people don't care about privacy." Young people in particular are said to have no interest in privacy. What's more, privacy just protects bad behavior because those of us with "nothing to hide have nothing to fear." And anyway, the argument goes, new privacy laws would be bad policy since "privacy is bad for business."

Professor of Law, Washington University. For their helpful comments, thanks to participants at the University of Alabama conference, Elizabeth Knoll, Greg Magarian, Evan Selinger, and Brian Tamanaha. Thanks also to my research assistants Ujjayini Bose, Matt Cin, Carolina Foglia, and Grace Corbett.

There are other common claims, but these four are perhaps the most common. They are also myths. Each of these four claims – (1) *Privacy Is Dead*, (2) *(Young) People Don't Care about Privacy*, (3) *People with Nothing to Hide Have Nothing to Fear*, and (4) *Privacy Is Bad for Business* – is either plainly false or deeply misleading. In this chapter, I'll explain why each of these four privacy claims is really a privacy myth. First, privacy cannot be dead because it deals with the rules governing personal information; in an age of personal information, rules about how that information can flow will be more important than ever. Second, people (even young people) *do* care deeply about privacy, but they face limited choices and limited information about how to participate in the processing of their data. Third, privacy isn't just for people with dark secrets; it's for all of us because information is power and personal information is personal power. Finally, privacy is not always bad for business. One of the best hopes for meaningful privacy protection in the future is for businesses to compete on privacy, and there is some evidence that this is starting to happen.

My goal here is not just to be contrary. Instead, I hope to clear away some of the confusion surrounding the way we talk about privacy in the digital age. When we do that, when we are clear about what privacy is and why it matters, we can start to talk constructively about the kinds of legal and social rules we want to govern personal information in the information age. Our understandings of privacy must evolve; we can no longer think about privacy as merely how much of our lives are completely secret or about privacy as hiding bad truths from society. Privacy must be understood as the rules we have as a society for managing the collection, use, and disclosure of personal information.

Our society is experiencing an information revolution as powerful and disruptive as the industrial revolution of the nineteenth century. We need to think and talk about how to harness this revolution's great power while minimizing as many of its costs as we can. Or we can continue to believe the myths about privacy. But if we do that, if we think about privacy as outdated or impossible, our digital revolution may have no rules at all, a result that will disempower all but the most powerful among us.

Privacy is dead

Privacy is dead. We all know that, right? We live in a society that is constantly generating vast quantities of personal information, which in turn is tracked, screened, and sorted by corporations and government entities.[1] Schools track student sleep and activity patterns,[2] CCTV (closed-circuit

---

[1] Daniel J. Solove, *The Digital Person: Technology and Privacy in the Information Age* (New York: NYU Press, 2005).

[2] Mary Shapiro, "Parkway's Use of Fitness Monitors Raises Privacy Questions," *St. Louis Post-Dispatch*, January 3, 2012, available at www.stltoday.com/suburban-journals/metro/education/parkway-s-use-of-fitness-monitors-raises-privacy-questions/article_af46b549-0f1e-5a41-8a26-7f77c91ced20.html.

television) cameras guard every street corner and traffic light,[3] and drones are starting to appear in our skies.[4] We're even tracking ourselves, using personal electronics such as GPS (Global Positioning System) watches, fitness trackers, and other gadgets that make the "quantified self" a realistic possibility.[5]

Academic and public commentators have long bemoaned the Death of Privacy. The last twenty years have seen the publication of innumerable books bearing variations on the titles "Privacy Is Dead" or "Privacy Is Dying."[6] At the launch of Sun Microsystems' Jini technology in January 1999, Sun's

---

[3] Julia Angwin, *Dragnet Nation* (New York: Times Books, 2014).

[4] M. Ryan Calo, "The Drone as Privacy Catalyst," *Stan. L. Rev. Online* 64 (2011), available at www.stanfordlawreview.org/sites/default/files/online/articles/64-SLRO-29_1.pdf.

[5] Gary Wolf, "The Data-Driven Life," *N.Y. Times Magazine* (April 28, 2010), available at www.nytimes.com/2010/05/02/magazine/02self-measurement-t.html?pagewanted=all&_r=0.

[6] For example, see Lori Andrews, *I Know Who You Are and I Saw What You Did: Social Networks and the Death of Privacy* (New York: Free Press, 2012); Ross Clark, *The Road to Big Brother: One Man's Struggle Against the Surveillance Society* (London: Encounter Books, 2009); Simson Garfinkel, *Database Nation: The Death of Privacy in the 21st Century* (Sebastopol, CA: O'Reilly, 2000); David H. Holtzman, *Privacy Lost: How Technology Is Endangering Your Privacy* (San Francisco: Jossey-Bass, 2006); *Index on Censorship, Privacy is Dead! (Long Live Privacy!)* (London: Sage 2011); Jeffrey Rosen, *The Unwanted Gaze: The Destruction of Privacy in America* (New York: Vintage, 2001); James B. Rule, *Privacy In Peril: How We Are Sacrificing a Fundamental Right in Exchange for Security and Convenience* (2009); Christopher Slobogin, *Privacy at Risk: The New Government Surveillance and the Fourth Amendment* (Chicago: Chicago Press, 2007).

CEO Scott McNealy famously declared, "You have zero privacy anyway. Get over it."[7] McNealy's outburst made headlines at the time and has outlived both the Jini technology and Sun's existence as an independent company. It continues to be quoted today by scholars, journalists, and industry figures.[8] More recently, Vint Cerf, a leading figure in the creation of the internet and Google's "Chief Internet Evangelist," suggested that privacy might be a historical anomaly. Facebook founder Mark Zuckerberg was more blunt, declaring that "the age of privacy is over."[9] Privacy is dead, or at the very least, it is dying.

But if privacy is dead (or dying), it is dying a very long, slow, and drawn-out death. Privacy's death throes (if that's really what they are) go back to at least 1890, the year in which anxiety about privacy in American law is typically first noted. In that year, East Coast elites were gripped by a kind of privacy panic motivated by changes in technology and

---

[7] Polly Sprenger, "Sun on Privacy: Get Over It," *Wired.com* (January 26, 1999), available at www.wired.com/politics/law/news/1999/01/17538.

[8] E.g., Bruce E. Boyden, "Regulating at the End of Privacy," *University of Chicago Legal Forum*, 173 (2013): 173; Orin Kerr, "Applying the Fourth Amendment to the Internet: A General Approach," *Stanford Law Review* 62 (2010): 1038; Paul Rosenzweig, "Privacy and Counter-Terrorism: The Pervasiveness of Data," *Case Western Reserve Journal of International Law* 42 (2010): 629; Jonathan Zittrain, "Privacy 2.0," *University of Chicago Law Forum* (2008): 68.

[9] Marshall Kirkpatrick, "Facebook's Zuckerberg Says the Age of Privacy Is Over," *Readwrite* (January 2, 2010), available at http://readwrite.com/2010/01/09/facebooks_zuckerberg_says_the_age_of_privacy_is_ov#awesm=~oo2UUoqssyO3eq.

society. In June, opera star Marion Manola obtained an injunction against a New York theatre promoter who wanted to publish a photograph of her wearing tights that had been taken on stage with one of the new cameras.[10] In July, E. L. Godkin, editor of *The Nation*, argued for what he termed "the right to privacy," a person's right "to decide how much knowledge of his personal thought and feeling, and how much knowledge, therefore, of his tastes and habits, of his own private doings and affairs, and those of his family living under his own roof, the public at large shall have."[11] And in December, Louis Brandeis and Samuel Warren's famous article "The Right to Privacy"[12] bemoaned the rise of gossip journalism and portable cameras and called for the creation of a tort to keep embarrassing true facts out of the newspapers.[13]

Legal historian Lawrence Friedman has shown how events like these were the result of elites feeling anxious that their dominant place in society was being threatened by a new democratic press using new tools to shine the light

---

[10] "Manola Gets an Injunction," *The New York Times* (June 18, 1890), 2; "Photographed in Tights," *The New York Times* (June 15, 1890), 2; see also Don R. Pember, *Privacy and the Press: The Law, the Mass Media, and the First Amendment* (Seattle: U. Washington Press, 1972), 56.

[11] E. L. Godkin, "The Rights of the Citizen: IV. To His Own Reputation," *Scribner's Magazine* 8 (1890): 65.

[12] Samuel Warren & Louis D. Brandeis, "The Right to Privacy," *Harvard Law Review* 4 (1890): 193.

[13] Neil M. Richards, "The Puzzle of Brandeis, Privacy, and Speech," *Vanderbilt Law Review* 63 (2010): 1295.

of publicity upon them.[14] But the attention to privacy took root in American law, and a body of privacy law began to develop.[15] This body of law protected a wide variety of interests, including intrusions into private places, the use of people's photographs for commercial purposes without consent, and disclosures of facts that were either embarrassing or portrayed a person in a "false light."[16]

Another privacy panic gripped the United States in the 1960s, as emerging computer technology began to allow the creation of "data banks" holding personal information. This digital privacy problem prompted a spate of books and cultural attention on the threat to privacy. With the public now aware of the rising importance of credit reporting bureaus and other uses of data in society, Congress passed the Fair Credit Reporting Act of 1970, and, following the Richard Nixon surveillance scandal, the Privacy Act of 1974. At the same time, some of the notions of privacy that Warren and Brandeis had suggested for matters of private law began to work their way into constitutional law as well. In a series of blockbuster cases, the US Supreme Court held that the US Constitution protected privacy interests in areas as diverse as police wiretapping,

---

[14] Lawrence Friedman, *Guarding Life's Dark Secrets: Legal and Social Controls over Reputation, Propriety, and Privacy* (Palo Alto: Stanford University Press, 2007).

[15] Neil M. Richards & Daniel J. Solove, "Prosser's Privacy Law: A Mixed Legacy," *California Law Review* 98 (2010): 1887.

[16] William Prosser, "Privacy," *California Law Review* 48 (1960): 383.

political group membership, contraceptives, abortion rights, and the possession of obscene pornography.[17]

There have been other privacy panics, but these two will do for my purposes here. Notice how each of these earlier privacy panics followed a similar pattern – new technologies and social practices threatened established social norms about how information could be used. This was followed by a great deal of soul searching, a sense of crisis, and then the gradual accommodation of the new practices through a combination of regulation, acceptance, and the passage of time. Privacy was threatened, and the threat was tamed, though each time norms shifted and the resulting society was less "private" than before, at least by the standards of the old social norms.

This brings us to the present day, in which we understand that another series of threats to privacy signals another Death of Privacy. The continued growth of digital technologies after the 1960s produced the personal computer boom of the 1980s, the web boom of the late 1990s, and the explosion of cell and smart phones in the 2000s. We are now witnessing the beginnings of the "Internet of Things," in which billions of electronic devices will connect to the internet, collecting and relaying unimaginably large amounts of data. At the same time, the terrorist attacks of 9/11 and 7/7, among others, have energized security services across the

---

[17] *Katz v. United States*, 389 U.S. 347 (1967); *NAACP v. Alabama*, 357 U.S. 449 (1958); *Griswold v. Connecticut*, 381 U.S. 479 (1965); *Roe v. Wade*, 410 U.S. 113 (1973); *Stanley v. Georgia*, 394 U.S. 557 (1969).

democratic world. Today we see levels of surveillance of the citizens of democratic societies that would previously have been politically and technically unimaginable. Edward Snowden and Glenn Greenwald's revelations about the scale of surveillance by the National Security Agency (NSA) have prompted a global debate about surveillance and privacy that has produced front-page news for over six months. But surely privacy is really dead now? Surely we face the end of any notions of privacy, right?

No. I'd like to suggest, to the contrary, that Privacy Is Not Dead. Privacy is one of the most important questions facing us as a society. Privacy is actually very much alive. But it all depends on what we mean by "privacy." Privacy can of course mean many things. If we mean merely "how much information people know about us," then privacy is shrinking. But this is a very narrow and unhelpful way of understanding privacy.

Let's take a step back from the Internet of Things and digital privacy Armageddon for a moment. Certainly, many of the kinds of things we call "privacy" aren't currently threatened by new digital technologies and are very much alive. At a general level, we still put locks on our houses, we still wear clothes, and we still use doors to keep the general public out of our bathroom and bedroom. We require the government to get a warrant before it enters our home and (NSA revelations notwithstanding) wiretaps our phone, and reads our mail (whether electronic or paper). We expect our lawyers and our therapists to keep our confidences in trust and expect our accountant and our bank to do the same with our financial details. We expect our doctors to do the same with information about our health, and while we realize that many of our health records are now electronic, we don't expect them to become available on a Google search or left lying carelessly around on a laptop at the airport. The fact that data breaches are newsworthy (and cause substantial personal, legal, and business harm) supports these expectations rather than diminishes them.

What about the argument that information technology is inevitably gobbling up privacy, causing the zone of our privacy to dwindle to almost nothing? To answer that question, let's look at our previous privacy panics. Warren and Brandeis were worried about gossip columnists and so-called "Kodakers lying in wait."[18] These phenomena still exist today, but they were managed by changes in law and social norms, and by the passage of time. Today, we have rules governing journalistic breaches (though in the United States such rules sometimes conflict with the First Amendment), and we have rules preventing stalking or overzealous tactics by the paparazzi. Similarly, commentators in the 1960s were worried by wiretapping, the creation of data banks, and the processing of personal data. Again, these phenomena exist today, but they have also been managed (at least in their pre-internet

---

[18] Robert E. Mensel, "'Kodakers Lying in Wait': Amateur Photography and the Right of Privacy in New York, 1885–1915," *American Quarterly* 43 (1991): 24.

forms) by changes in the law and social norms, and by the passage of time. I'd like to suggest that our ongoing worries about the Death of Privacy (privacy's century-old melodramatic death throes) are really an ongoing social and legal conversation about how to manage some of the costs caused by changes in information technologies.

If we think about privacy as the *scope* of information we can keep completely secret or unknown, then that kind of privacy is certainly diminishing. We are living through an information revolution, and the collection, use, and analysis of many kinds of personal data are inevitable. But if we think about privacy as the question of what *rules* should govern the collection and use of personal information, then privacy has never been more alive. In fact, it is perhaps the most important and most vital issue we face as a society today.

Reflecting this broader understanding, legal scholars use the term "privacy" to mean at least four kinds of legal rules governing (1) invasions into protected spaces, relationships, or decisions; (2) the collection of information; (3) the use of information; and (4) the disclosure of information. In his leading conceptual work on privacy, Daniel Solove has taken these four categories and expanded them to an occasionally bewildering sixteen categories, including surveillance, interrogation, aggregation, and disclosure. These understandings are much broader than the scope of how much personal information is being recorded, and they ask not merely how much information is being collected, but how it might be used and retained, and what limits might be placed on such use and retention.[19]

As our information revolution develops, and new things become possible, we will likely develop new categories of privacy. We will certainly need new rules for the many new ways that information is being and will be used. But it's important not to forget that we have many such rules already. Some of these rules are ones that we typically think of as "privacy rules." For example, tort law governs invasions of privacy including peeping (or listening) Toms,[20] the unauthorized use of photographs for commerce,[21] and the disclosure of sexual images without consent.[22] Some states also protect against criminal invasions of privacy, as the prosecution of Dharun Ravi for recording Tyler Clementi's private sexual activities illustrated.[23] The Fourth Amendment requires that the government obtain a warrant before it intrudes on a "reasonable expectation of privacy," and is backed up by a complex web of federal and state laws regulating eavesdropping and

---

[19] Daniel J. Solove, *Understanding Privacy* (Boston: Harvard University Press 2008).

[20] *Hamberger v. Eastman*, 206 A.2d 239 (N.H. 1964).

[21] *Agence France Presse v. Morel*, 769 F. Supp. 2d 295 (S.D.N.Y. 2011); For the use of another's name, voice, signature, photograph, or likeness for advertising or selling or soliciting purposes, see Cal. Civ. Code § 3344 (West) (2013).

[22] *Lee v. Penthouse International, Ltd.*, CV96-7069SVW (JGX), 1997 WL 33384309 (C.D. Cal. Mar. 19, 1997).

[23] N.J. Stat. Ann. § 2C:14–9 (West 2004); *State of New Jersey v. Ravi*, 2011 WL 1512060 (N.J. Super. 2011).

wiretapping by both government and private actors.[24] In addition to the Privacy Act and the Fair Credit Reporting Act, federal laws regulate the collection and use of financial information, medical and genetic information, and video privacy, among others.[25] States, led by California, have also added privacy protections, such as California's constitutional right of privacy (applicable to private actors), reading privacy laws, data breach notification statutes, and the recent spate of laws prohibiting employers from asking for the social media account passwords of their employees.[26]

We have other rules that regulate the use of information that we might not typically think of as privacy rules. For example, civil rights law prohibits (among other things) the use of sensitive information such as race or gender to make hiring or promotion decisions.[27] Patent law regulates the use

---

[24] *Katz v. United States*, 389 U.S. 347 (1967); Electronic Communications Act of 1986, 18 U.S.C. §§ 2510–2522 (1986); California Penal Code § 632(a).

[25] Health Insurance Portability and Accountability Act of 1996, 42 U.S. C. § 300gg and 29 U.S.C § 1181 *et seq.* and 42 USC 1320d et seq. (1996); Gramm-Leach-Bliley Financial Services Modernization Act of 1999, 15 U.S.C. §§ 6801, 6809, 6821, 6827 (1999); Video Privacy Protection Act, 18 U.S.C. § 2710 (1988).

[26] Cal Const. Art. I, § 3(b)(3); Reader Privacy Act, West's Ann. Cal. Civ. Code §§ 1798.90 (2012); Disclosure of breach of security of computerized records, N.J. Stat. Ann. § 56:8–163 (West)(2013); Request for access to social networking account prohibited N.M. Stat § 21-1-46 (2013).

[27] Title VII of the Civil Rights Act of 1964, 42 U.S.C. § 2000e *et seq.* (1964).

of information to design and build products – indeed, intellectual property law in general is all about regulations of the use of information.[28] Trade secret law allows companies to restrict access to private commercial information and grants remedies for breaches of such commercial privacy.[29] Even the First Amendment, long thought of as the enemy of privacy, is a kind of information rule that mandates the circumstances in which other laws cannot restrict certain free flows of information, such as the publication of true and newsworthy facts by journalists, or truthful and non-misleading advertisements for lawful products.[30]

Taking this broader perspective on "privacy" reveals that our society has some very surprising advocates for privacy. In fact, the very institutions that are usually thought of as opposing privacy for individuals often use law to secure privacy for their institutional operations. For example, consider Facebook, long thought of as being antithetical to privacy as a result of its encouragement to everyone to "share" as much of their personal information as possible to as many people as possible. But even Facebook cares about privacy. Visitors to its campus (including its employees) are required to sign non-disclosure agreements, by which they agree to keep

---

[28] *Eldred v. Ashcroft*, 537 U.S. 186, 216 (2003).

[29] See generally Roger M. Milgrim, *Milgrim on Trade Secrets* (New York: Lexis, 9th ed., 2011).

[30] Neil M. Richards, "Why Data Privacy Law Is (Mostly) Constitutional," *William & Mary Law Review* (forthcoming, 2014), available at SSRN: http://ssrn.com/abstract=2335196.

confidential any information they learn on their visit. At a news conference at its Seattle offices recently, Facebook personnel reportedly tried to get journalists to sign a non-disclosure agreement before they could attend.[31] The National Security Agency – indeed, the entire national security apparatus – is similar. While the NSA and other security agencies accumulate vast amounts of sensitive personal information in the United States and abroad, they insist on vast amounts of privacy for their own operations. This includes the secret Foreign Intelligence Surveillance Court, the "gag orders" placed upon recipients of National Security Letters and orders pursuant to section 215 of the Patriot Act, and many other legal measures. Indeed, the only reason the public knows about many of the NSA's surveillance activities is as a result of leaks by Edward Snowden and others, which almost certainly violated laws and agreements crafted to preserve the operational privacy of the national security apparatus.

My purpose in these examples is not to pick on these organizations. On the contrary, when used appropriately, privacy rules such as trade and government secret protection can advance important social interests. I am trying instead to make a point that is easy to overlook: when the very entities that are used as exemplars of the "Death of Privacy" use suites of robust legal tools to preserve their own privacy, it

---

[31] Elana Zak, "Facebook Asks Reporters to Sign Non-Disclosure Agreement," *10,000 Words* (January 26, 2012, 6:14 PM), available at www.mediabistro.com/10000words/facebook-asked-reporters-to-sign-non-disclosure-agreement_b10303.

makes no sense to claim that privacy is dead. In fact, these examples rather show that privacy is a complex phenomenon, and that we should be talking about the balance between different kinds of privacies and different rules for managing flows of information rather than privacy's demise. When viewed from this perspective, neither Facebook nor the NSA reject privacy; on the contrary, they have complicated relationships with privacy, embracing (like so many other people and institutions) privacy for themselves but offering somewhat less privacy for others, especially where they have institutional incentives to make money or protect government interests. Put this way, the real question isn't whether privacy is dead, but rather when privacy is appropriate, and who benefits from this allocation.

Thus, when we expand our idea of "privacy" beyond embarrassing secrets to include the regulation of information flows more generally, we see that privacy – and privacy law – is very much alive. Privacy law is one of the fastest-growing fields of legal practice. Indeed, as a legal specialty, privacy law is booming. Thousands of law firms in the United States alone advertise their privacy practices.[32] The International Association of Privacy Professionals (IAPP), the privacy industry's largest professional group, currently has more than 12,000 members, an increase of nearly 3,000 just since

[32] Martindale, http://www.martindale.com/Find-Lawyers-and-Law-Firms.aspx, Practice Area Search term: "Privacy Law" (last searched on November 16, 2013).

the beginning of 2012.[33] The IAPP itself attributes the exponential growth of the privacy profession to several factors, including that many different kinds and sizes of organizations are employing "Chief Privacy Officers" or other privacy professionals in order to manage the legal and other responsibilities that come from holding increasingly large amounts of personal data on customers, employees, and others.[34] In two influential studies, Kenneth Bamberger and Deidre Mulligan have documented both the establishment of the professional corporate privacy officer, the emergence of the Federal Trade Commission as a powerful regulator of consumer privacy, and the development of substantive notions of privacy by corporate professionals that contradict any suggestions of a Death of Privacy.[35]

The important point I want make here is this: however we define privacy, it will have to do with information. And when we think of information rules as privacy rules (as we

---

[33] Alec Foege, "Chief Privacy Officer Profession Grows with Big Data Field," *Data Informed* (February 5, 2013), available at http://data-informed.com/chief-privacy-officer-profession-grows-with-big-data-field.

[34] International Association of Privacy Professionals, "A CALL FOR AGILITY: The Next-Generation Privacy Professional" (May 15, 2010), available at www.huntonprivacyblog.com/uploads/file/IAPP_Future_of_Privacy.pdf.

[35] Kenneth A. Bamberger & Deirdre K. Mulligan, "Privacy on the Books and on the Ground," *Stanford Law Review* 63 (2011); Kenneth A. Bamberger & Deirdre K. Mulligan, "Privacy in Europe: Initial Data on Governance Choices and Corporate Practices," *George Washington Law Review* (forthcoming 2014).

have in many cases for a very long time), we can see that digital technologies and government and corporate practices are putting many existing notions of privacy under threat. But privacy in general isn't dying. This is because privacy is the shorthand we have come to use to identify information rules. If we were designing things from scratch, we would probably want to use a different term than "privacy" ("information" springs to mind, as does the accurate but unexciting European term "data protection"). But in the English-speaking world at least, "privacy" is so deeply rooted as the word we use to refer to the collection, use, and disclosure of information that we are probably stuck with it, for better and for worse.

The idea that Privacy Is Dead is thus a myth. Certain kinds of privacy may fade or become obsolete, but this is natural, because privacy is usually the product of social norms, and social norms change over time and across societies. Nineteenth-century notions of privacy are dead, but so, too, is everyone from the nineteenth century.[36] Yet the need for rules governing the uses of information persists. Legal and social rules that govern how information about us is obtained and used (broadly defined) are always necessary, and the information revolution is increasing the importance of these rules rather than decreasing them. Some of these

---

[36] At the time of writing, there are only five people on Earth verified to have been born before 1900. Wikipedia, "Oldest People," available at https://en.wikipedia.org/wiki/Oldest_people#Ten_verified_oldest_people_living (last accessed November 19, 2013).

rules will require hard choices, but a hard choice is a vital choice.

Seen from this perspective, privacy is vital, too. It is very much alive. Privacy isn't dead. Rather, privacy is inevitable.

People don't care about privacy

But even if the reports of privacy's death have been exaggerated, surely it is true that few ordinary people care about privacy any more. Or at least young people have given up on privacy, right? The exponential growth of social networks such as Facebook and Twitter, in which users share increasing amounts of personal information, the rise of "sexting," and the perceived willingness of us all to trade our personal information for convenience and safety all seem to suggest that public interest in privacy is on the decline. More pointedly, many observers have suggested that because young people have eagerly embraced digital technologies and social networks, they care even less about privacy than older generations.[37]

There is some empirical evidence to back up such notions. A 2013 government study of British internet users[38] suggested that British adults have become less concerned about online

---

[37] Janet Kornblum, "Online privacy? For young people, that's old-school," *USA Today* (October 22, 2007), available at http://usato day30.usatoday.com/tech/webguide/internetlife/2007-10-22-online-privacy_n.htm.

[38] OfCom, "Adults' media use and attitudes report" (2013), available at: http://stakeholders.ofcom.org.uk/binaries/research/media-liter acy/adult-media-lit-13/2013_Adult_ML_Tracker.pdf.

privacy over the past decade; whereas 70 percent of those surveyed in 2005 were concerned about online privacy, now only 52 percent responded similarly. Of course, 52 percent is still a majority, and it is difficult for surveys to probe exactly what "concerned about privacy means" – whether it is a fear that one's name and address is vaguely "out there" or a more nuanced concern about the effects of databases being used to profile, sort, and nudge consumers and citizens towards behaviors corporations and governments might desire.

Privacy is notoriously difficult to define, and this definitional looseness no doubt contributes to ambiguity in consumer surveys. When asked whether they care about privacy, are consumers thinking about the fact that their tweets can be read by the world, the fact that Google is serving ads to them based upon a transcript of their web-surfing, or the fact that the government is logging the recipients of all their emails and telephone calls? This imprecision is reflected in other surveys finding that consumers do care about online privacy, and that they are often unaware of issues such as Do Not Track or the protections afforded by privacy law. Several studies suggest that consumers believe that privacy law is more protective of them than is actually the case; for example, one prominent study showed that most consumers incorrectly believe that websites with privacy policies cannot share data about them without their consent.[39]

---

[39] Chris Jay Hoofnagle & Jennifer King, "What Californians Understand about Privacy Online" (September 3, 2008), available at http://papers.ssrn.com/sol3/papers.cfm?abstract_id=1262130.

Nevertheless, there does seem to be some truth to the idea of a "privacy paradox": the idea that people indicate a concern about privacy in general, but then act in ways that might seem contradictory; for example, by selling their personal information very cheaply in practice.[40] There could be several explanations for this discrepancy. Consumers could be misled by the terms of transactions in which they hand over their data. They might undervalue the risks of over-sharing data, or of the value of their data, especially in contexts where a "free" service is offered in exchange. They might be coaxed by highly persuasive interfaces that use sophisticated testing models to be as effective as possible, or which limit their ability to make meaningful choices about their privacy.[41] Or it may simply be that while consumers sincerely value their privacy in the abstract, in the bustle of their everyday lives the bewildering need to check and re-check privacy settings can be too much. This latter explanation suggests that the regime of "privacy self-management" – the idea that consumers must manage a system of dense privacy policies, hidden opt-outs, and ever-changing settings – might be a failure, and that we need something better to

[40] Patricia A. Norberg, Daniel R. Horne, & David A. Horne, "The Privacy Paradox: Personal Information Disclosure Intentions versus Behaviors," *Journal of Consumer Affairs* 41(1) (2007): 100–126.

[41] Pam Dixon & Robert Gellman, *Online Privacy: A Reference Handbook* (2011), e-book, accessed September 24, 2013, available at http://wustl.eblib.com.libproxy.wustl.edu/patron/FullRecord.aspx?p=766988: 15–16.

replace it.[42] This could be a generally applicable consumer privacy law like virtually every other democracy has, or it could be more specific default rules that track consumer expectations. There is certainly substantial anecdotal and empirical evidence to support the proposition that consumers are bewildered and concerned by the difficulties of managing their privacy in practice.[43] One notable study found that merely to read all of the privacy policies an average internet user encounters in a year would take 76 work days.[44] Thus, while more study of this is certainly needed, the "privacy paradox" is thus more likely a symptom of our ineffective system of privacy management than anything else.

Of course, the trump card in the People Don't Care about Privacy argument is young people. Even if older people, the argument goes, care about privacy, our young generation of

[42] Daniel J. Solove, "Privacy Self-Management and the Consent Dilemma," *Harvard Law Review* 126 (2013): 1880.

[43] Mary Madden & Aaron Smith, "Reputation Management and Social Media," *Pew Internet & American Life Project* (May 26, 2010), available at http://www.pewinternet.org/Reports/2010/Reputation-Management/Summary-of-Findings.aspx, 6; McGraw Hill Financial Global Institute, "Consumers: Losing Control of Online Privacy" (October 30, 2013), available at http://www.mhfigi.com/societal-trends/consumer-concerns-about-data-privacy.

[44] See Aleecia M. McDonald & Lorrie Faith Cranor, "The Cost of Reading Privacy Policies," *I / S: A Journal of Law and Policy for the Information Society* 4 (2008): 540; see also Alexis C. Madrigal, "Reading the Privacy Policies You Encounter in a Year Would Take 76 Work Days," *The Atlantic* (March 1, 2012), available at www.theatlantic.com/technology/archive/2012/03/reading-the-privacy-policies-you-encounter-in-a-year-would-take-76-work-days/253851.

digital natives certainly doesn't. Young people growing up with digital communications technologies care much less about privacy, with their lives shared, tweeted, and Instagrammed extensively.[45] One journalistic account of young people's privacy preferences expressed this sentiment aptly:

> Kids today. They have no sense of shame. They have no sense of privacy. They are show-offs, fame whores, pornographic little loons who post their diaries, their phone numbers, their stupid poetry – for God's sake, their dirty photos – online. They have virtual friends instead of real ones. They talk in illiterate instant messages. They are interested only in attention – and yet they have zero attention span, flitting like hummingbirds from one virtual stage to another.[46]

As the CEO of Disney put it more succinctly, when it comes to privacy, "kids don't care ... they can't figure out what I'm talking about."[47]

---

[45] Shea Bennett, Tumblr, Facebook, Twitter, Instagram & Snapchat – How Teens Use Social Media [INFOGRAPHIC], All Twitter: The Unofficial Twitter Resource (October 18, 2013), available at www.mediabistro.com/alltwitter/teens-social-media_b50664.

[46] Emily Nussbaum, "Kids, the Internet, and the End of Privacy: The Greatest Generation Gap since Rock and Roll," *New York Magazine* (February 12, 2007), available at http://nymag.com/news/features/27341.

[47] Gina Keating, "Disney CEO Bullish on Direct Web Marketing to Consumers," *Reuters* (July 23, 2009), available at www.reuters.com/article/2009/07/23/us-media-disney-idUSTRE56M0ZY20090723?pageNumber=1&virtualBrandChannel=0.

It may be trendy to talk anecdotally about young people who seem not to care about privacy, but there is a substantial body of evidence demonstrating that it, too, is a myth. Young people *do* care about privacy; in fact, they often are much more sophisticated about privacy – and digital privacy – than their elders. Young people do look at privacy differently, but those differences as much as anything else reflect their sophistication about the importance of practical privacy management in their lives. In their study of young people's attitudes toward privacy, Hoofnagle et al. found that young people care as deeply about privacy as their elders and that they might even be more vigilant and more likely to engage in privacy-protective behaviors (such as supplying false information) than older people.[48] There is further empirical evidence that young people are more likely to engage in sophisticated tweaking of the privacy settings they are given on social networks than older people.[49]

Young people might certainly share information about themselves that shocks their elders,[50] but young people

---

[48] Chris J. Hoofnagle, Jennifer King, Su Li, & Joseph Turow, "How Different Are Young Adults from Older Adults When It Comes to Information Privacy Attitudes and Policies?" *Social Science Research Network* (2010), available at SSRN: http://ssrn.com/abstract=1589864 or http://dx.doi.org/10.2139/ssrn.1589864, 10.

[49] A. Marwick, D. Murgia-Díaz, & J. Palfrey, "Youth, Privacy and Reputation (Literature Review)," *Berkman Center Research Publication* 5 (2010): 33.

[50] J. Henley, "Are teenagers really careless about online privacy?" *The Guardian* (October 21, 2013), available at www.theguardian.com/technology/2013/oct/21/teenagers-careless-about-online-privacy.

sometimes doing risky things to shock old people has been the defining characteristic of youth culture for the past fifty years. In reality, young people care deeply about privacy, but they care about privacy in a different way that reflects their outlook on life. Sociologists danah boyd and Alice Marwick explain that young people's concern about privacy is less about privacy against their peers and much more about privacy against the perceived authority figures in their lives – their parents, teachers, and (for older ones) potential employers.[51] By contrast, young people enthusiastically embrace electronic platforms as a way to meet like-minded young people, to experiment with identity, to create a social space defined by young people and not by adult parents and teachers, and because they see the benefits of connectivity, including the small chance that they might "go viral" or become a micro-celebrity.[52] Although some of these goals require the sharing of sometimes intimate personal information with others, none of them necessarily equate to a lack of concern with privacy. Indeed, in their engagement in the processes of "boundary management" with multiple publics, boyd and Marwick suggest that young people are both more concerned with privacy than older people and

---

[51] danah boyd & Alice E. Marwick, "Social Privacy in Networked Publics ..." (conference paper, 2011), available at: http://papers.ssrn.com/sol3/papers.cfm?abstract_id=1925128.

[52] *Ibid*; see also Alice Marwick et al., "Youth, Privacy and Reputation" (2010): 13.

they have a more sophisticated understanding of the nuances of information flows in digital social environments.[53]

Why, then, if young people care deeply about privacy, have some journalistic and popular accounts of young people's privacy preferences focused on their apparently privacy-denying behavior? One explanation is that young people frequently engage in risky behavior with a diminished sense of the likelihood of negative future consequences. From this perspective, why should risky privacy behavior be any different from other risky behaviors including sex, alcohol and drugs, or reckless driving? We don't think that driving laws should be abolished simply because some people (including some young people) drive recklessly, after all. Another explanation is that the social networks that teens and other young adults encounter are engineered by default to be more public. From this perspective, all people, including young people, have a range of limited choices when it comes to privacy. In their study of young people's engagement with social networks, boyd and Marwick explain that social dynamics in the physical world are typically "private-by-default, public-through-effort."[54] It is difficult to get to know people in the physical environment, and personal information requires effort to obtain. But by contrast, in an online environment in which social networking companies have a financial incentive to maximize the amount of personal

[53] *Ibid.*

[54] dannah boyd & Alice E. Marwick, "Social Privacy in Networked Publics" (2011): 10.

information that is disclosed (in order to sell more and better advertisements), the model of privacy is public-by-default, private-through-effort. Faced with such radically altered default settings and a limited range of choices, it should thus be no surprise that young people appear to be less privacy-conscious.

As with the Death of Privacy, a closer look at public attitudes towards privacy shows that the reality is far more complicated than the simple mantra that people no longer care about privacy. A more accurate interpretation of the available evidence suggests that people do in fact care about privacy, but they are bewildered by the difficulty of protecting their personal information in a time of rapid technological change and limited options. Indeed, the myth that People Don't Care about Privacy suggests a kind of reverse privacy paradox – if people really don't care about privacy, why do they talk about it so much? After all, if we didn't really care about privacy, it wouldn't be regular front page news, books on privacy wouldn't sell, and it would not be a major topic of public debate.

More fundamentally, the debate about whether people do or do not care about privacy obscures a much more important point: in the English-speaking world, we use the word "privacy" to capture our anxiety about many of the changes that the digital revolution has enabled. I argued in response to the myth that Privacy Is Dead that we should think about "privacy" as more than merely nineteenth-century fears of unwanted publicity. When we think about privacy more broadly as the ability of people to participate in how their personal information is collected, processed, and used, it becomes clear that people (including young people) definitely care about this problem. They care deeply about it, because it is one of the defining questions of our age.

If you have nothing to hide, you have nothing to fear

How people understand privacy is crucially important to understanding a third myth about privacy, which is the oft-repeated belief that People with Nothing to Hide Have Nothing to Fear. According to this view, privacy is no more than the ability to hide unpleasant truths about ourselves from the public. And it follows from this assumption that privacy is only for those of us with dark secrets. It is the protection for a misbehaving minority, a kind of false advertising of one's character and reputation. As Richard Posner famously put it, privacy is no more than a person's "right to conceal discreditable facts about himself."[55]

But the Nothing to Hide argument is a myth. Most of the time, it is just false. More importantly, though, it is a misleading way of thinking about the issues that privacy raises in digital societies. It frames the question of privacy in ways that ignore the reasons why privacy matters. And it does this in three separate ways.

[55] Richard A. Posner, *Economic Analysis of Law* (New York: Aspen, 5th ed., 1998): 46.

First, all of us have "something to hide," or at least information that we don't want to have broadcast to the world. Few people would be comfortable with having images of their activities in the bedroom or bathroom made public, even where those activities are common to all or to many. In particular, the disclosure of facts or images about our naked bodies or sex lives would be psychologically catastrophic to many people. Rutgers University freshman Tyler Clementi infamously jumped to his death from the George Washington Bridge when his roommate shared a video stream of him being intimate with another person in his dorm room.[56] And as cameras become ubiquitous (and also a part of many people's sex lives),[57] the growth of "revenge porn," in which (usually) men disclose videos of their former lovers engaged in sex acts, has become a national problem. As legal scholar Danielle Citron puts it, "[r]evenge porn is as harmful to the person who shared intimate photos with a trusted loved one as the person whose picture was taken by someone else and then disclosed without consent. Sharing

[56] Neil M. Richards, "The Limits of Tort Privacy," *Journal of Telecommunications & High Technology Law* 9 (2011): 357; Ian Parker, "The Story of a Suicide," *The New Yorker* (February 6, 2012), available at http://www.newyorker.com/reporting/2012/02/06/120206fa_fact_parker.

[57] Jonathan Freedland, "Are Smartphones Causing a Bonking Crisis?" *The Guardian* (November 26, 2013), available at http://www.the guardian.com/commentisfree/2013/nov/26/smartphones-bonking-crisis-british-less-sex-technology.

sensitive information with a confidante does not waive one's privacy expectation in the information."[58]

Another category of information many people would want to keep secret is their intellectual activities, especially their tastes in books or films. Reading and thinking are the core of a free society, and the foundation for a robust exercise of First Amendment rights.[59] Thus, when Judge Robert Bork was nominated to the Supreme Court in 1987, his controversial belief that there was no right to privacy caused an enterprising reporter for the Washington City Paper to find and publish his movie-watching history.[60] While the most embarrassing movie on Bork's account was John Hughes' *Sixteen Candles*, the episode caused Congress to pass the Video Privacy Protection Act. Congress no doubt feared the disclosure of more salacious titles rented by members of the House and Senate – fears that the selective disclosure of their intellectual pursuits might cause people to be judged out of context.

More generally, intellectual privacy such as that afforded by movie or reading privacy protections is an important civil liberty. It allows us mental breathing space to experiment

---

[58] Danielle Keats Citron, *Hate Crimes in Cyberspace* (Boston: Harvard University Press, forthcoming 2014): ms. 143.

[59] Neil M. Richards, *Intellectual Privacy* (New York: Oxford University Press, forthcoming 2014).

[60] Michael Dolan, "The Bork Tapes Saga," *The American Porch: An Informal History of an Informal Place*, available at http://theamericanporch.com/bork2.htm. See generally Neil M. Richards, "The Perils of Social Reading," 101 *Georgetown Law Journal* 689 (2013).

with unpopular, dangerous, or even deviant ideas, from politics, to sex, to religion. Many people who fear that their intellectual activities are being monitored will restrict them to the mainstream, the conventional, and the boring. Such self-censorship has effects not only on what people read but on what they write and say. For example, one recent survey of over 500 American writers found that the fear of government surveillance had caused many of them to curtail what they read, write, and say.[61] And when writers are chilled in their own liberties of thinking and expression, society as a whole is deprived of the insight of their views.

Mere surveillance of our reading can be used to deter, but disclosure of those habits can also be used to discredit or destroy. In late 2013, the *Huffington Post* reported that the US government was monitoring the web-surfing habits of clerics and academics who spoke about their radical Islamic beliefs. Although the subjects of surveillance were speakers and not terrorists, data on their preferences in pornography was being collected in order to disclose it and thereby discredit them. One enthusiastic supporter of this policy argued that "dropping the truth on them" was better than dropping a bomb on them.[62] Of course, democratic governments aren't allowed to censor speakers they disagree with (much less

[61] "Chilling Effects: NSA Surveillance Drives Writers to Self-Censor," *PEN America* (November 12, 2013), available at http://www.pen.org/sites/default/files/Chilling%20Effects_PEN%20American.pdf.

[62] Glenn Greenwald et al., "Top-Secret Document Reveals NSA Spied On Porn Habits As Part Of Plan To Discredit 'Radicalizers,'" *The*

bomb them). But the threat of disclosure of embarrassing reading habits can be used to censor indirectly. Such a threat is not limited to terrorists or radical speakers, particularly if surveillance of reading habits or political views by governments or private actors is widespread.[63] If we care about vibrant public debate, we must care about intellectual privacy. After all, in a free society, there is no such thing as a bad (or even a discreditable) idea.[64]

A second reason why the Nothing to Hide argument is misleading is that it reduces privacy to an individual's right to hide big secrets. Such a crude reduction of the issue ignores both the complexity of privacy, as well as the social value that comes from living in a society that not everything about us is publicly available all of the time. This is the insight of legal scholar Daniel Solove in his book *Nothing to Hide*. Solove shows how thinking of privacy as the hiding of discreditable secrets by individuals is a mistake because privacy is about more than hiding secrets, and can mean a wide variety of things. He notes that privacy is "often eroded over time, little bits dissolving almost imperceptibly until we finally begin to notice how much is gone."[65] Privacy, in his view, is a social

Huffington Post (November 26, 2013), available at http://www.huf fingtonpost.com/2013/11/26/nsa-porn-muslims_n_4346128.html.

[63] Neil M. Richards, "The Perils of Social Reading," *Georgetown Law Journal* 101 (2013): 689.

[64] Neil M. Richards, "Intellectual Privacy," *Texas Law Review* 87 (2008): 387.

[65] Daniel J. Solove, *Nothing To Hide: The False Tradeoff Between Privacy and Security* (New Haven: Yale 2011): 30.

value rather than merely an individual one. Rather than thinking about privacy as simply the individual right to hide bad deeds, we should think more broadly about the kind of society we want to live in. A society in which everyone knew everything about everyone else would be oppressive because it would place us all under the glare of publicity all the time; there would be no "free zones for individuals to flourish [in]."[66] Legal scholar Julie Cohen goes further, arguing that privacy is necessary for humans to be able to decide who they are. In Cohen's account, our selves are fluid, constantly being built and changed by our activities, thoughts, and interactions with other people. Privacy, in her view, shelters the development of our dynamic selves "from the efforts of commercial and government actors to render individuals and communities fixed, transparent, and predictable." Privacy protects our ability to manage boundaries between ourselves and others so that self-determination is possible.[67] It helps us avoid the calculating, quantifying tyranny of the majority. Privacy is thus essential for individuality and self-determination, and has substantial benefits for society.

Third, reducing privacy to an individual's right to hide dark secrets ignores the power effects of privacy. Information is power, and knowing information about someone gives power over them – the power to blackmail, persuade, and

[66] *Ibid.*, 50.
[67] Julie E. Cohen, "What Privacy Is For," *Harvard Law Review* 126 (2013): 1905.

classify. Let's take blackmail first. As the example of the NSA porn surveillance reveals, secrets can of course be used to blackmail or silence someone. Such occurrences are regrettably common, even in democratic societies. As I have written elsewhere, the Federal Bureau of Intelligence's surveillance of Martin Luther King, Jr.'s communications produced evidence of marital infidelity that it used to blackmail him.[68] But blackmail can occur beyond the secrets we want to hide. "Revenge porn" nude or sexual images are often used to blackmail or silence former lovers. Even non-embarrassing personal information, such as financial information or account passwords, can be a threat in the wrong hands. None of these is a dark secret we want to hide, but the revelation of any of them or the threat of identity theft can be used for blackmail purposes.

More fundamentally, small or large collections of personal information can be used to persuade others to do our bidding. Businesses that hold a lot of information about us can market to us more persuasively, potentially reaching us at a moment of weakness when our guard is down. Such practices might not be illegal under current law; indeed, depending on one's view of consumer rights, they might also be unproblematic from a policy perspective. But they certainly change the power relationships between those who hold personal information and the subjects of that data.

[68] Neil M. Richards, "The Dangers of Surveillance," *Harvard Law Review* 126 (2013): 1934.

Existing consumer protection law is based upon the idea that certain kinds of power differentials can be problematic in the marketplace, which is why we require labeling and ingredient lists, and forbid practices such as redlining, coercive installment contracts,[69] negligence waivers,[70] or coercive company stores.[71] Consumer protection law forbids not just deceptive acts, but those that are unconscionable – acts that are characterized by a lack of meaningful choice on the part of the consumer or by a gross inequality in bargaining power.[72] Consumer profiles backed by so-called "big data analytics" enable exactly this kind of enhanced persuasion. This is something I have elsewhere called the "Power Paradox" of big data – big data analytics are powerful, but that power is

---

[69] *Williams v. Walker-Thomas Furniture Co.*, 350 F.2d 445 (D.C. Cir. 1965).

[70] *Tunkl v. Regents of the U. of Cal.*, 383 P.2d 441 (Cal. 1963).

[71] Price J. Fishback, "Did Coal Miners Owe Their Souls to the Company Store?" *Journal of Economic History* 46 (1986): 1101. This type of practice has been outlawed by laws such as Ohio Rev. Code Ann. § 4113.18 (West)(2013).

[72] See for example, Kan. Stat. Ann. § 50–627 (West) (2013) (forbidding suppliers from taking "advantage of the inability of the consumer reasonably to protect the consumer's interests because of the consumer's ... ignorance, ... inability to understand the language of an agreement or similar factor"); Idaho Code Ann. § 48–603C (West) (2013) (permitting the court to take into account "whether the alleged violator knowingly or with reason to know, induced the consumer to enter into a transaction that was excessively one-sided in favor of the alleged violator" when determining if an act, practice, or method is unconscionable).

typically wielded by those who are already powerful.[73] Communications scholar Joseph Turow makes a similar point – while our new digital technologies are usually framed as giving us enhanced choice, the reality is very different. Businesses using consumer profiles that most people don't know exist can tailor content to persuade and influence those people, often without them knowing about it.[74]

The persuasive effects of data-based marketing have not been limited to commerce, and have started to influence the political process. The Obama Campaign was feted after the 2012 presidential election for its use of data-based analytics in targeting its campaign advertising, outreach, and other efforts. Spearheaded by University of Chicago data scientist Rayid Ghani, the campaign used publicly available data from voter records to plot the electorate on a grid and employed analytic techniques to segment the electorate, assessing how likely each voter was to vote for Obama and Romney, and then assessing them for persuadability.[75] On the one hand, the use of new technologies by political campaigns is nothing new. But on the other, the use of these new technologies to

[73] Neil M. Richards & Jonathan H. King, "Three Paradoxes of Big Data," *Stanford Law Review Online* 66 (2013): 41, available at http://www.stanfordlawreview.org/sites/default/files/online/topics/66_StanLRevOnline_41_RichardsKing.pdf.

[74] Joseph Turow, *The Daily You: How the New Advertising Industry Is Defining Your Identity and Your Worth* (New Haven: Yale 2012).

[75] Jonathan H. King, "The New Washington Data Grid," *jhking.com* (September 16, 2013), http://jhking.com/2013/09/16/the-new-washington-data-grid.

segment, sort, identify, and persuade voters heralds a new kind of political persuasion, one based upon targeting and data rather than speaking and canvassing. Surely banning the use of data by campaigns would be impossible as a practical (or likely a constitutional) matter. It might not even be good policy even if we could. But my point is to highlight the increased persuasive power that data-based analytics give to already powerful entities – advertisers, corporations, political machines, and government entities. Assessing the degree to which these developments are a problem is impossible if we think about privacy or information rules as only hiding discrete pieces of discreditable information about ourselves.

The segmenting power of data analytics suggests a third power effect that personal data can enable – the power to sort. In an influential 1993 book, sociologist Oscar Gandy described the digital privacy revolution as ushering in something he called "The Panoptic Sort."[76] Gandy used this term to describe the use of large datasets by government and private bureaucracies to classify, assess, and sort individuals for analysis and control – a system of power based upon personal information. Turow has also illustrated the even more powerful sorting ability that two decades of computer and data science have enabled. Today, personal data is used to classify and sort us all.[77]

[76] Oscar H. Gandy, *The Panoptic Sort: A Political Economy of Personal Information* (Boulder: Westview Press 1993).
[77] Turow, "The Daily You ... "

On the one hand, the increased efficiency of sorting enabled by the information revolution has many useful applications. Large-dataset analytics have many powerful applications that don't even use personal data, such as weather and traffic forecasting, the design of better automotive components, spell-checkers, and search engines.[78] Analytics based on personal data are useful, too, enabling better decisions in the medical, credit, and insurance contexts, and possibly some prevention of terrorism and other crimes.[79] But this increased power to sort can be used for bad or morally ambiguous purposes as well. Lawyers have another word for this kind of sorting, which is "discrimination." Consider the use of consumer profiles to determine the likelihood we would buy products at a given price. Such relatively simple analytic techniques could enable a website (say, like Amazon.com) in which all prices were optimized to the highest value we might be willing to pay. Sophisticated analytics could also raise the spectre of a new kind of "redlining" – the denial or discrimination of services to people on the basis of race or other suspect criteria. Of course, predictive analytics need not use race directly; they could be designed to ignore

[78] Viktor Mayer-Schönberger & Kenneth Cukier, *Big Data: A Revolution That Will Transform How We Live, Work, and Think* (New York: Houghton Mifflin, 2013).

[79] Omer Tene & Jules Polonetsky, "Privacy in the Age of Big Data: A Time for Decisions," *Stanford Law Review Online* 64 (2012) 63, available at http://www.stanfordlawreview.org/sites/default/files/online/topics/64-SLRO-63_1.pdf.

race and use other variables that correlate with race. Or perhaps such algorithms might not use race indirectly, but impose a brutal individualized economic rationalism upon us all as consumers and citizens.

Thankfully, the strong form of that society is not upon us yet, but some of its weaker cousins are. And if we dismiss the problems caused by privacy or personal data as nothing more than bad people hiding bad deeds, we will miss the transformative power effects of the digital revolution entirely. For better or worse, we use the term "privacy" as a shorthand to capture all of the issues raised by personal data. As a result, privacy is not just for those of us with something to hide. Of course, we all have something to hide. But more fundamentally, questions of privacy include many of the most fundamental questions of civil liberties and economic and political power in a digital society. From that perspective, privacy is for everyone.

Privacy is bad for business

Let's say you agree with me so far. Let's concede for purposes of argument that privacy is alive, that people care about it, and that it's broader than hiding discreditable information. All this means is that the choice to protect privacy is a policy choice; it is a choice that we could make, but it is also one that we need not make. It's at this point in debates about privacy that the policy trump card gets played: privacy might be something people want, but it's bad for business. Privacy gets in the way of technological innovation; it's a kind of tax on progress. We have a free internet built on personalized advertising, which requires that businesses know about the people surfing the web. We also have all sorts of free mobile applications and other services that are paid for by eyeballs. If we stopped or slowed the free flow of personal information, our digital revolution could grind to a halt. As a result, Privacy Is Bad for Business.

At the outset, there are a few problems with this claim, such as the idea that maybe our information policy shouldn't be entirely geared towards what is good for business. But let's talk about the "free" internet first. We hear a lot about the "free" internet, and "free" apps and services. Consider Facebook's promise, featured prominently on its web sign-up page, that "It's free and always will be."[80] Of course, Facebook isn't really "free." Consumers don't pay money to use the Facebook service, but they can't use it without giving Facebook the right to collect and use often vast amounts of valuable personal information about them. Facebook collates and uses such personal information to target advertisements to its users. It encourages its users to share information about themselves, and those users are then sold to Facebook's real customers, its advertisers. Some observers have termed this arrangement "digital sharecropping" rather than "free stuff."[81]

---

[80] Facebook, www.facebook.com.

[81] For example, Nicholas Carr, "The Economics of Digital Sharecropping," *RoughType.com* (May 4, 2012), available at http://www.roughtype.com/?p=1600.

But however we characterize it, when personal information is bartered for access (whether users know that or not), an economic exchange is taking place. When that's happening, it's misleading to call such services "free." In fact, there is good evidence from the behavioral sciences that calling something "free" tends to cause consumers to make irrational choices, overvaluing the benefits of "free" goods and ignoring the costs.[82]

Debunking the idea of the "free" internet is important because it shows the extraordinary economic value of personal information. Much of the popular rhetoric of the internet suggests that nothing much of value is transferred by users. Any individual piece of personal data may have minimal value, but vast amounts of tiny value add up. Indeed, the sheer size of internet fortunes based upon personal information demonstrates this point nicely. Facebook's Initial Public Offering was valued at US$ 104 billion, and its only real assets were its users, their data, and their eyeballs as viewers of advertising.[83] One recent study estimated that each user's data is worth US$ 98 to Facebook, roughly equivalent to the value of users of LinkedIn (US$ 93) and Twitter

---

[82] For example, Kristina Shampa'ner, Nina Mazar, & Dan Ariely, "Zero as a special price: The true value of free products," *Marketing Science* 26 (2007) 742, available at http://people.duke.edu/~dandan/Papers/PI/zerofree.pdf and Chris Jay Hoofnagle & Jan Whittington, "The Price of 'Free': Accounting for the Cost of the Internet's Most Popular Price," *UCLA Law Review* (forthcoming 2014).

[83] Andrew Tangel & Walter Hamilton, "Stakes are high on Facebook's first day of trading," *The Los Angeles Times*, May 17, 2012.

(US\$ 110).[84] So rather than thinking about the internet as a group of services provided for free, we should think of it as it really is – as a collection of companies making money from personal information that has substantial value.

This brings us back to the idea that Privacy Is Bad for Business or is anti-innovation. From a narrow perspective, requiring businesses to account for privacy might make things more expensive. After all, if personal information collected or harvested from users is valuable, restrictions on what information businesses can collect or how they can use it would cut into profits. If Facebook, Twitter, or LinkedIn had to pay their users even a fraction of what their data was worth, they would get very expensive very quickly. From this perspective, privacy rules are a kind of tax on both innovation and profitability. This is a common refrain heard from business groups. (A perhaps flippant response to this argument is that paying employees fairly for their labor is also a kind of a tax on profitability, but one that the law requires.)

More fundamentally, viewing privacy rules as a tax ignores the importance of trust in the digital environment. Customers share their data with companies under the expectation that it will be treated ethically and responsibly. There is good evidence that consumers share because they think that privacy law is considerably more protective than it

[84] George Anders, "A Twitter User Is Worth \$110; Facebook's \$98; LinkedIn's \$93," *Forbes.com* (November 7, 2013), available at http://www.forbes.com/sites/georgeanders/2013/11/07/a-twitter-user-is-worth-110-facebooks-98-linkedins-93.

really is, for example, that the existence of a privacy policy means that personal information will not be shared or sold to others without their actual consent.[85] There is also evidence that the presence of privacy controls in computer interfaces makes individuals more likely to share their personal information.[86] This is an insight that has a long pedigree in our legal system. Some of our oldest privacy rules, including the duties of professional confidentiality, reflect an understanding that trust promotes the sharing of information. I have elsewhere called this idea the *information-sharing function of confidentiality*.[87] To get better medical, legal, or other advice, we need to tell the truth, to share fully and frankly. But because information is power, sharing information frequently puts us at the mercy of our confidante, who can use this information to their benefit or our detriment. Confidentiality solves both

---

[85] Chris Jay Hoofnagle & Jennifer King, "Research Report: What Californians Understand About Privacy Offline," *Social Science Research Network* (May 15, 2008), available at http://papers.ssrn.com/sol3/papers.cfm?abstract_id=1133075; Chris Jay Hoofnagle & Jennifer M. Urban, "Alan Westin's Privacy Homo Economicus," 49 *Wake Forest Literature Review* (forthcoming 2014).

[86] Laura Brandimarte et al., "Misplaced Confidences: Privacy and the Control Paradox," Presentation at *Workshop on the Economics of Information Security: Negative Information Looms Longer than Positive Information* (June 14, 2011), available at http://www.futureofprivacy.org/wp-content/uploads/2010/09/Misplaced-Confidences-acquisti-FPF.pdf.

[87] Neil M. Richards, "The Perils of Social Reading," *Georgetown Law Journal* 101 (2013): 689.

problems, letting us get better advice and protecting us from being taken advantage of by our confidantes.[88]

Confidentiality protects our professional confidences as well, though this is a feature of confidentiality that is easy to overlook. To stay with the example of doctors and lawyers, their client confidentiality – privacy – rules are thus a huge asset to confiders and confidantes, professionals and their clients. They are an elegant solution to the fact that information is power. That solution is the insight that confidentiality of information promotes trust, reliance, and investment in the relationship. Confidentiality rules help to guarantee that the professional won't abuse the power difference with her client. And the information-sharing function of confidentiality encourages more information to flow to the professional, allowing him or her to provide better advice. Confidentiality thus promotes trust and improves the quality of the professional services on offer. The very word "confidentiality" implies this double meaning, for when we share a *confidence* we trust our confidante; quite literally, we have *confidence* in their discretion.

No doubt because of these mutually beneficial features, confidentiality rules are well-established in the older information professions such as law, medicine, librarianship, the priesthood, and psychology. They are starting to take root in our newer information professions as well. As noted earlier, the past decade has seen the rise of the Chief Privacy Officer

[88] *Ibid.*

(CPO), a senior executive responsible for managing the legal and other risks of a company's personal information management policies. The rise of the CPO has also been reflected in the remarkable growth of organizations such as the Future of Privacy Forum and the larger International Association of Privacy Professionals. The IAPP's mission is to help "organizations manage and protect their data," and its members include CPOs at large and small corporations, partners at law firms, and general counsel at companies of various sizes. Scholars studying the rise of the CPO position have concluded that CPOs (and privacy professionals more generally) self-consciously fulfill an important regulatory role within companies even in the absence of formal legal rules for the management of personal information.[89] They conclude that much of the impetus for the creation of internal mechanisms and professionals to manage information practices is the privacy expectations of their own customers. As one leading privacy professional puts it, from a CPO's perspective "[t]he end objective in my mind is always what's the right thing to do to maintain the company's trusted relationship with our employees, with our clients, with any constituency in society that has a relationship to us, which is probably pretty much any constituency."[90]

[89] Kenneth A. Bamberger & Deidre K. Mulligan, "Privacy on the Books and on the Ground," *Stanford Law Review* 63 (2011): 249–254, available at http://www.stanfordlawreview.org/print/article/privacy-books-and-ground.

[90] *Ibid.*, 271.

At the same time, privacy also represents an opportunity for companies on which they can compete with each other by innovating on privacy and trust. A recent American Civil Liberties Union report suggests ways in which a demonstrable commitment to privacy and other ethical information processing practices is essential for the long-term sustainability of technology companies. According to the report, which relies on case studies of corporate privacy practices, companies that safeguard their users' privacy can "increase use and consumer spending" and "generate positive press and create customer loyalty."[91] The report also notes the insight of Bamberger and Mulligan, that even though legal safeguards in the United States for personal information currently lag behind technological advances, customers expect (and often demand) that the businesses with which they deal engage in ethical custodianship of their personal information. The report concludes that "[a]s consumers become more aware of the consequences of online activity and are faced with an ever-expanding array of options, they will increasingly demand products that are not only innovative but also protect their privacy," and notes that the relative maturation of the digital technology sector presents companies with an opportunity to innovate and compete on privacy grounds.[92]

[91] Nicole A. Ozer & Chris Conley, "Privacy & Free Speech: It's Good for Business," *ACLU of Northern California* (2nd ed. 2012), available at http://aclunc-tech.org/files/privacy_free_speech_good_for_business.pdf

[92] *Ibid.*, 27.

The importance of privacy as customer trust has been illustrated most clearly by the effect of the Snowden revelations on the goodwill of the American technology industry. One of the earliest and most controversial revelations by *The Guardian* was that most of the major US cloud and internet companies had been participating in the National Security Agency's PRISM program, under which they shared large amounts of customer information with the government.[93] Some smaller technology companies closed their doors rather than participate in what they considered to be such an egregious breach of user trust. Ladar Levison, the owner of secure email company Lavabit, halted the operations of his company and posted an open letter to his customers suggesting that he had been forced to disclose the contents of customer emails to the government.[94] Another secure communications provider, Silent Circle, also shut down its email service, stating that it had "not received subpoenas, warrants, security letters, or anything else by any government," but that it was acting preemptively before it was forced to adhere to such

---

[93] Glenn Greenwald & Ewen MacAskill, "NSA Prism program taps in to user data of Apple, Google, and others," *The Guardian* (June 6, 2013), available at http://www.theguardian.com/world/2013/jun/06/us-tech-giants-nsa-data.

[94] Lavabit, http://lavabit.com (last visited October 24, 2013). See also Michael German, America, "NSA Surveillance is Bad for Business," *ACLU* (August 13, 2013), available at https://www.aclu.org/blog/national-security-technology-and-liberty/america-nsa-surveillance-bad-business (quoting open letter on lavabit.com).

requests.[95] With trust undermined by seemingly unfettered US government access, American technology companies started to lose the trust of their users, especially those users in other countries. The technology giants got the message, and within a few months of the Snowden revelations began to advocate and lobby for limitations on government surveillance of their users. In an open letter of their own, a website, and advertisements in major newspapers, eight of the leading internet companies, led by Google and Microsoft, spoke out against government surveillance. As the general counsel of one of the companies put it aptly, "people won't use technology they don't trust."[96]

The Snowden revelations, of course, involve government surveillance, rather than data collection and use by the companies themselves. And it is precisely because large internet companies collect and retain so much personal information that government security services so eagerly look to access their servers. But the Snowden affair reveals that companies are beginning to understand how important customer trust is to their businesses, and how integral privacy rules – the ethical collection and use of personal information – are to

[95] Michael German, "America, NSA Surveillance is Bad for Business," *ACLU* (August 13, 2013), available at https://www.aclu.org/blog/national-security-technology-and-liberty/america-nsa-surveillance-bad-business.

[96] Edward Wyatt & Claire Cain Miller, "Tech Giants Issue Call for Limits on Government Surveillance of Users," *New York Times* (December 9, 2013), B1.

those businesses. Along with the rise of the CPO and a broader ethical sensibility with respect to personal data, it also suggests that privacy will be a space in which competitive innovation can occur among businesses in the future. Just as the information trade and data analytics have been a spur to innovation, allowing services such as Google search, Amazon.com, and Pandora, so can the need to engage in ethical and trust-promoting information processing spur the kind of innovation needed to take advantage of the undeniable benefits of our new information technologies while minimizing their equally undeniable social costs.

Conclusion

In this chapter, I have tried to show that privacy – the ways individuals participate in data about them – isn't dead. In fact, privacy is one of the most important issues facing modern information societies. How we shape the technologies and data flows will have far-reaching effects for the social structures of the digital societies of the future. Even the decision to do nothing about these new technologies is a decision, whether it is made as a matter of policy, a misguided understanding of constitutional rights, or technology-induced paralysis. If the law, social norms, or the market do not regulate privacy, engineers writing code in Silicon Valley or elsewhere will.[97] Our technological trajectory is not natural

[97] See Lawrence Lessig, *Code and Other Laws of Cyberspace* (New York: Basic 1999).

or inevitable; either way, it will be the product of many individual human choices about how those technologies are built.

But how we understand the problem, how we frame privacy matters.[98] Framing privacy as a regressive attempt to hide embarrassing secrets is very different from other frames such as the extent to which ordinary people will be able to participate in the ways their data is used. Unfortunately, much of the public and legal debate about privacy has been clouded by misleading (and sometimes self-serving) myths about what privacy is and why it matters. Clearing away these myths reveals the scope of the challenge that faces us – crafting rules for the collection and flow of personal information that balances the values of privacy, autonomy, security, and profitability, among others. But in a democratic information society, the basic rules of information flows should be made through public deliberation rather than technocratic isolation. Clearing away the myths about privacy is an important first step.

[98] Woodrow Hartzog, "The Fight to Frame Privacy," *Michigan Law Review* 111 (2013): 1021.

2

The Yes Men and *The Women Men Don't See*

Rebecca Tushnet

A mericans seem to care more in practice about privacy as against their neighbors than they do about privacy as against their governments. As a result, they often take steps to protect privacy-as-against-neighbors that are completely ineffective against government or corporate tracking: the Gmail account Batman906 enables its owner to speak in many ways that are invisible to her friends and family, which is what she wants, even though Google knows all about her – including the link between Batman906 and her work email.[1]

---

[1] See danah boyd, *It's Complicated* (New Haven: Yale University Press, 2014), 56 (most people seek privacy against those who hold power over them; teens in particular don't worry about governments and corporations, but about parents, teachers, and other immediate threats); cf. A. Michael Froomkin, "Anonymity and Its Enmities," *Journal of Online Law* 4 (1995) (distinguishing "whether and how

It's in this citizen-on-citizen context that I want to talk about pseudonymity, its abuses, and its promises. Law tends to see anonymity and pseudonymity in the same way: both serve as a shield against suppression, often suppression by private parties. But the two types of self-presentation have distinct features. Pseudonymity can also be creative and valuable in itself, though this is less often recognized in the law. I want to give an account of pseudonymity that considers both what pseudonymity protects and what it enables. The positive aspects of pseudonymity include both insulation from certain pressures, allowing self-development and exploration, and also the ability to build a community of like-minded souls.

It's a cliché that the internet allows people to try on new identities, liberating themselves but potentially harming others. Anonymity is the usual target of critiques of such identity-play: anonymity is often used for sexual and racial harassment, suppressing the very liberatory potential that disconnection from physical identity was supposed to offer. These accounts, while offering powerful examples of the misuse of expression disconnected from identifiable people, often set up a binary opposition between a persistent identity linked to legal names and pure anonymity.[2] Pseudonymity

an author identifies herself" and "whether and how the real identity of the author can be determined by others"); David Post, "Pooling Intellectual Capital: Anonymity, Pseudonymity, and Contingent Identity in Cyberspace," *University of Chicago Legal Forum* (1996) (distinguishing anonymity, pseudonymity, and traceability).

[2] Nancy Leong, in a departure from this general trend, points out that there are pseudonymous harassers who use a persistent online

is just a variant of anonymity in these critiques, and dedicated harassers often switch pseudonyms so they can continue their attacks.

Catharine MacKinnon has argued that appeals to "privacy" regularly serve to preserve private (generally white and male) power over others, whose oppression is therefore seen as none of the state's business. Some scholars have updated this critique to now focus on the privacy of anonymous/pseudonymous users. While most of those scholars recognize that anonymity has valid uses, especially for critics of powerful institutions, they emphasize the harms that anonymous harassers can cause. They also rightly point out that, often, anonymous/pseudonymous harassers can dish it out but they can't take it – their harassment identifies specific people, often women, and tries to deny their targets the privacy and dignity that the harassers claim exclusively for themselves.[3]

identity, which she characterizes as "trying to have it both ways. That is, they are trying to have the benefits that come with having a known identity – the community recognition; the ability to form relationships with others; the claim to speak authoritatively on certain topics – as well as the benefits associated with anonymity – namely, the ability to avoid any consequences for racist and misogynistic comments in real life." Nancy Leong, "Consequences and Conclusions," *Feminist Law Professors* (December 17, 2013), available at http://www.feministlawprofessors.com/2013/12/consequences-conclusions.

[3] Martha Nussbaum & Saul Levmore, eds., *The Offensive Internet: Speech, Privacy, and Reputation* (Cambridge: Harvard University Press, 2011).

For example, Violentacrez, a prolific distributor of "upskirt" photos and other content featuring sexualized young girls, operated under the principle that women who went out in public had to expect that pictures of their breasts and legs would appear online. He ultimately lost his job when a reporter connected his online identity to his real name – producing outraged responses from defenders of his "privacy."[4] The story shows how pseudonymity can support male privilege: the condition of being looked at can do great harm to women, while the ability to *not* be seen provides great benefits to men. (It also highlights that pseudonymity is almost always relative – the government, and often anyone with a sufficient interest in investigating, can generally dig up enough information to connect an online identity with a legal identity. But most people, most of the time, nonetheless act as if their pseudonyms are separate.)

Because the debate over the absence of "real names" online has often, and legitimately, focused on the gendered nature of the harms at issue, I would like to offer a feminist account of some of the affordances of pseudonymity. Pseudonyms offer one way for people to maintain boundaries between different aspects of their identities, but without isolating themselves. Identity management can be particularly important to people

---

[4] Adrian Chen, "Reddit's Biggest Troll Fired From His Real-World Job; Reddit Continues to Censor Gawker Articles," *Gawker* (October 15, 2012), available at http://gawker.com/5951987/red dits-biggest-troll-fired-from-his-real-world-job-reddit-continues-to-censor-gawker-articles.

in vulnerable circumstances – those constrained by gender, race, job, family, or community from expressing certain beliefs or interests to their usual acquaintances.

Using a name that most people with whom you interact understand is not your legal name can create rich communities and interactive works of art. Talking about such spaces may help elucidate why proposals to require "real names" in online interactions can seem so threatening not just to free speech in the abstract, and not just to people living under oppressive regimes who fear being thrown in jail or worse for speaking out, but also to the ordinary, everyday project of the creation of the self. Pseudonymity may also provide another way for the law to acknowledge that privacy is not binary – shared with no one or shareable with everyone. The practice of maintaining separate, persistent identities is not inherently disreputable or suspect even in liberal democracies.

The two cultural artifacts from which my title comes illustrate the way the stakes in anonymity and pseudonymity can differ, often influenced by gender. The Yes Men are pranksters who impersonate powerful figures for political ends.[5] Impersonation is often illegal, under trademark and other laws, but courts have found it protected by the First Amendment in the specific instance of nonprofit

[5] The Yes Men take their name from a cliché for people (men) who agree with whatever a more powerful person says. As a side note, it may be relevant to a feminist analysis that a man who says "yes" doesn't have the same implied sexual/romantic meaning that "a woman who says yes" does ("she said yes!").

impersonation designed to highlight and criticize an impersonated organization. This is consistent with Supreme Court precedent that allows a speaker to take on a pseudonym that implies, perhaps misleadingly, that she's part of a larger group.[6] The Yes Men use impersonation to exercise power over media narratives and to seize attention for themselves as the fake unravels.

The Women Men Don't See is the title of an award-winning science fiction story by James Tiptree Jr., a pseudonym for Alice Sheldon.[7] It is an account, from a male perspective, of two ordinary women – denigrated as unattractive by the narrator – who decide to leave the planet with aliens. There's nothing they individually can do about misogyny and male dominance, so they opt out. (According to one of them, hating men would be "like hating the weather." There's no point in being angry, but also no point in staying.) In this context, not being seen, being invisible, and being misread as a man are all forms of defensive power – not power over others, but protection from the exercise of power by men. Pseudonymity is a way of participating instead of opting out, but still remaining unseen.[8]

---

[6] The court wrote in terms of "anonymity" as a First Amendment right, but the speaker actually adopted a pseudonym that implied she was speaking for a larger group of citizens in *McIntyre v. Ohio Elections Comm'n*, 514 U.S. 334, 342 (1995).

[7] Julie Phillips, *James Tiptree, Jr.: The Double Life of Alice B. Sheldon* (New York: Picador, 2007).

[8] Maintaining identity separation also serves self-protective purposes for fans – fellow fans don't know their legal identities, and family

These two experiences of pseudonymity, legal and cultural, suggest ways in which pseudonymity can cushion against the exercise of social power. While Tiptree's female characters opted out, Tiptree did not, and like the Yes Men was able to engage in a biting critique of existing arrangements. Pseudonymity is a kind of control over discourse about one's self, even if it's vulnerable to a focused investigation; separating identities by contexts remains valuable even in a pervasively surveilled society.

Pseudonymity, impersonation, and the law

As Laura Heymann has explained, US law accommodates pseudonymity in a variety of ways, including allowing pseudonymous litigation and facilitating name changes even when that makes it harder for other people to attribute previous actions to the newly-named person or entity.[9]

members, colleagues, etc. don't know their fandom activities, so there is a separation in both directions; keeping distinct identities allows fans to preserve freedom in their online expression. Raeleen V. Damian, "Fanonymity: an investigation of motivations for being anonymous in online fandom," Master's thesis, California State University, Fullerton (2007).

[9] Heymann says that "[n]ame or trademark changes that make it more difficult for others to retrieve information about the person or entity are not legally prohibited, even though such changes can result in increased search costs, and even though others may have been induced to act in a way in which they would not have acted if they had known about the person's or the company's history." Laura A. Heymann, "Naming, Identity, and Trademark Law," *Indiana Law Journal* 86 (2011): 437–442.

Impersonation of someone else who actually exists, however, can often be made illegal – at least, where it is likely to do harm. The most obvious example comes from trademark law. A counterfeiter pretending to be the original committing not just a tort, but a crime.[10] This is true even if the counterfeiter's direct customers understand that they're buying fakes. The harm comes later, when other people think the products are real and therefore overpay or overtrust their performance. Recent Supreme Court precedent suggests that some sort of harm is constitutionally required before lies can be criminalized, but the Court was willing to assume that ordinary trademark infringement was sufficiently harmful to pass the constitutional threshold.[11]

And yet this leaves significant potential for lawful impersonation: impersonation that is unbelievable to any reasonable person, or whose harms can't plausibly be translated into short-term economic or physical terms. This probably includes satire, method actors getting into character, poets using hyperbole, and other "creative uses of knowingly false speech."[12] In significant part because of the expansion of trademark law and its cousin, right of publicity law, courts have increasingly been confronted

---

[10] 18 U.S.C. § 2320.

[11] *United States v. Alvarez*, 132 S. Ct. 2537 (2012).

[12] In its opinion, later affirmed by the Supreme Court, the 9th Circuit characterized these instances of speech, as well as other examples, as "highly protected." *United States v. Alvarez*, 617 F.3d 1198, 1213 (9th Cir. 2010), aff'd, 132 S. Ct. 2537 (2012).

with legal challenges to this kind of conduct. In these cases, the First Amendment offers protections to people who take on others' names.

For example, the Yes Men have been described as a "front" for artists "that create the illusion that they are an unstoppable army of anarchistic interventionists." The illusion is part of the message, similar to the mob/large group imagery employed by the online quasi-anarchists Anonymous. The artists' pseudonym is often itself concealed by the Yes Men's initial claims to speak for a corporate entity, such as the Chamber of Commerce. "'We use this language because it is so effective,' says Frank Guerrero, [a] Yes Men pseudonym. 'We think that by adopting the language, mannerisms, legal rights and cultural customs of corporations we are able to engage them in our own terms, and also perhaps to reveal something about how absurd it can get.'"[13] Notable Yes Men interventions include appearances at the World Trade Organization, as well as on BBC World News in the guise of Dow Chemical Company, accepting responsibility for the Bhopal disaster, causing Dow's share price to fall more than 2 percent, or US$ 4 billion in market value.[14]

---

[13] Kembrew McLeod & Rudolf Kuenzli, "I Collage, Therefore I Am: An Introduction to Cutting Across Media," in *Cutting Across Media: Appropriation Art, Interventionist Collage, and Copyright Law*, eds. Kembrew McLeod & Rudolf Kuenzli (Durham: Duke University Press, 2011): 1, 16–17.

[14] Sonia K. Katyal, "Semiotic Disobedience," *Washington University Law Review* 84 (2006): 489, 505–506.

Because the Yes Men lie about their identities in order to get public attention for their causes, one might think there would be legal remedies for their conduct. The Chamber of Commerce indeed sued the Yes Men for trademark infringement for impersonating official Chamber of Commerce representatives and claiming that the Chamber had reversed its position on climate change legislation. However, the Chamber dropped the suit before the Yes Men's First Amendment defense could be resolved.[15]

When a fake "Koch Industries" website and press release subsequently appeared, news organizations quickly recognized the hoax, but also reported on it. The materials purported to announce a decision by Koch to stop funding organizations that deny climate change; observers speculated that the website came from the Yes Men, or someone trained by them.[16] Koch, like the Chamber of Commerce, sought to unmask the legal identities of the person or people behind the website, who called themselves Youth for Climate

---

[15] The Electric Frontier Foundation described the Chamber's threats and lawsuit on its website. Electronic Frontier Foundation, "Chamber of Commerce v. Servin," available at https://www.eff.org/cases/chamber-commerce-v-servin, accessed January 12, 2014. Lisa Ramsey also described the impersonation. Lisa P. Ramsey, "Brandjacking on Social Networks: Trademark Infringement by Impersonation of Markholders," *Buffalo Law Review* 58 (2010): 851, 900.

[16] The Yes Men have "set up a hoaxers' training college, called Yes Lab, to 'help progressive groups carry out Yes-Men-style projects on their own.'" "Koch-ups and conspiracies," *The Economist* (December 13, 2010, available at http://www.economist.com/blogs/newsbook/2010/12/anti-business_protests.

December 10, 2010   Contact: Kate Anderson
kate.anderson@koch-inc.com
281-305-8418

KOCH INDUSTRIES ANNOUNCES NEW ENVIRONMENTAL COMMITMENTS

WICHITA, Kan. – Koch Industries remains committed to environmental responsibility and stewardship, announcing today that it will restructure its support for organizations that undertake climate change research and advocacy.

Since its founding, Koch Industries has been focused on achieving environmental excellence and using resources efficiently. Through extensive and award-winning efforts and investments, Koch Industries has implemented innovative practices that reduce energy use and greenhouse gas emissions in the manufacture and distribution of our products.

Based on recent internal evaluations of Koch Industries priorities, the company will be restructuring its support of climate change research and advocacy initiatives and will discontinue contributions to groups whose positions on climate change no longer match those of the company's leadership, beginning in January 2011.

Koch Industries is proud of its charitable history, particularly with regard to organizations such as Americans for Prosperity, Fraser Institute, Foundation for Research on Economics and the Environment, the Manhattan Institute for Policy Research, and the George C. Marshall Institute. These organizations have done much important work to advance science and policy on the issue of climate change.

However, based on a recent internal and thorough company review, Koch Industries has decided that its best course forward includes a discontinuation of funding for these

Figure 1 Fake "Koch Industries" web page

Truth (though they didn't call themselves that on the fake website or press release, which only identified Koch).

A federal court rejected both Koch's arguments for de-pseudonymizing the creators and Koch's claims for their liability under trademark and related laws. The defendants copied the look of the actual Koch Industries website; this was deliberate impersonation designed to fool audiences, at least until they'd thought about it for a bit. In ordinary trademark law, this would be infringement – possibly even counterfeiting. But here the products at issue were ideologies, not handbags. The court ruled that the defendants' use of the Koch trademark was therefore not a commercial use made "in connection with goods or services," as required to trigger trademark liability.[17] Precisely because the defendants didn't use the site to promote themselves in any way, including by soliciting donations, they were insulated from the otherwise broad sweep of trademark law. Mere interference with Koch's own ability to control its reputation and communicate its preferred messages was insufficient to infringe. Trademark protects the identification of the source of goods and services, not the source of ideas.

At the same time, the court emphasized that major media outlets hadn't been fooled by such an abrupt and implausible change in political orientation. The fact that some people might momentarily be fooled, or at least distracted, by the spoof wasn't enough reason to suppress it. In this way, the court linked the boundaries of trademark law to a broader conception of free speech. We often tolerate deceptive and misleading political speech both because we want citizens to sort things out themselves and because we fear a government with the power to suppress speech at the behest of other political actors.

The *Koch* case involves the most blatant impersonation blessed by a court as a matter of trademark law, but the

---

[17] *Koch Industries, Inc. v. Does*, No. 10-cv-01275, 2011 WL 1775765, at *3 (D. Utah May 9, 2011).

result is not unique. A few years earlier, for example, *Highfields Capital Management, L.P. v. Doe* protected a user's pseudonym "highfieldcapital" on a message board discussing the stock performance of a firm in which Highfields Capital Management held shares. Given the content of the message, which disparaged Highfields' skill, the court found insufficient evidence of commerciality, as opposed to criticism, to justify applying trademark law. The court also protected the user's legal name from disclosure to Highfields. "[A] person like defendant has a real First Amendment interest in having his sardonic message reach as many people as possible – and being free to use a screen name of the kind he used here carries the promise that more people will attend to the substance of his views."[18] In other cases, courts have increasingly refused to bar the use of a trademark owner's name, or a close variation thereon, as a domain name when the associated website's content is obviously critical.[19]

A separate body of law, the right of publicity, protects a celebrity's ability to exploit the commercial value of his or her identity regardless of confusion. Courts have extended this to cover use of celebrity impersonators in advertisements.[20] In addition, many works of art, from Andy Warhol's prints to Joyce Carol Oates' romans a clef, are both sold for profit and

[18] 385 F. Supp. 2d 969, 980 (N.D. Cal. 2005).

[19] One such case is *Lamparello v. Falwell*, 420 F.3d 309 (4th Cir. 2005).

[20] One decision covering the use of celebrity impersonators is *Allen v. National Video, Inc.*, 610 F. Supp. 612 (S.D.N.Y. 1985).

also reference celebrity identities. Unfortunately, courts have considered attempts to profit sufficient to bring such art within the scope of the right of publicity, absent some defense, and their attempts to define appropriate defenses have often produced bad results. One of the most popular tests for separating protected speech from actionable exploitation looks to "transformativeness": whether the artist has added anything of value to the work other than an accurate depiction of the celebrity.

Recently, a court found that a rapper performing as Ricky Ross, who adopted a well-known criminal's name and persona as a drug dealer, didn't violate the criminal's right of publicity because the new music the rapper created in that persona was creative and valuable in itself.[21] True, his music was based on the criminal's persona, and his lyrics referred to "his" criminal empire and cocaine-derived wealth, but these topics were merely the raw materials from which his performance was synthesized, not the sum and substance of his work. "He was not *simply* an imposter seeking to profit solely off the name and reputation of Rick Ross ... Using the name and certain details of an infamous criminal's life as basic elements, he created original artistic works."[22] The court further opined that the rapper was "a highly altered, essentially fantasized version of plaintiff," and his music could be

---

[21] *Ross v. Roberts*, – Cal. Rptr. 3d —, No. B242531, 2013 WL 6780578 (Ct. App. Dec. 23, 2013).

[22] *Ibid.*, *6 (emphasis added).

"analogized to a work of fiction in which the protagonist bears some resemblance to the original Rick Ross."

Notably, the case did not focus on whether anyone might have thought that the two people were actually the same person – the former criminal perhaps discovering a second career as a performer – though trademark law might have deemed Ross' new name and persona "explicitly misleading."[23] Misleadingness wasn't relevant to the plaintiff's cause of action because the right of publicity does not require consumer confusion as an element, as trademark infringement does. As a result, the transformativeness defense led the court to ask only whether the performer's version of the criminal added any new creativity. Because the criminal hadn't been a rapper, the rapper's new music insulated him from liability. Using the persona as a cloak and creating new expression, like a kid playing dress-up and inventing new adventures (or even retelling old ones), led to First Amendment protection.

But if "[w]e are what we pretend to be, so we must be careful about what we pretend to be,"[24] what does it mean to

---

[23] In criminal cases, prosecutors routinely present rap lyrics as autobiographical. Erik Nielsen & Charis E. Kubrin, "Rap lyrics on trial," *The New York Times*, January 13, 2014, A27 ("Even when defendants use a stage name to signal their creation of a fictional first-person narrator, rap about exploits that are exaggerated to the point of absurdity, and make use of figurative language, prosecutors will insist that the lyrics are effectively rhymed confessions. No other form of fictional expression is exploited this way in the courts.").

[24] Kurt Vonnegut, *Mother Night* (New York: Random House, 1961), v.

pretend to be someone else, even if that pretense is protected by the First Amendment? Legal scholars have extensively theorized anonymity, and also looked at some varieties of pseudonymity, but generally in less depth. The effects of adopting a new name and identity can differ substantially from the effects of being anonymous/unidentified, but much legal analysis nonetheless treats pseudonymity as a subset or special case of anonymity.[25] And this is true even though

---

[25] Lee Tien, "Who's Afraid of Anonymous Speech? McIntyre and the Internet," *Oregon Law Review* 75 (1996): 117, 167, 172–185. "[A]bsent anonymity, an author may feel constrained by her class, her gender, or her professional status, or by the ideas or opinions of her employer. An author of erotic stories, for example, may prefer to keep her identity as a high school physics teacher secret – perhaps because of potential retaliation from her employer, but also because of the potential for embarrassment and breakdown of classroom discipline that may otherwise result." Lyrissa B. Lidsky & Thomas F. Cotter, "Authorship, Audiences, and Anonymous Speech," *Notre Dame Law Review* 82 (2013): 1537, 1572–1573. Without reputational capital built up over time, "there is indeed no meaningful difference between anonymity and pseudonymity." David G. Post, "Pooling Intellectual Capital: Thoughts on Anonymity, Pseudonymity, and Limited Liability in Cyberspace," *University of Chicago Legal Forum* (1996), 139, 152. Victoria Smith Ekstrand discusses a model of anonymity as based in the degree of unknownness of a source. Victoria Smith Ekstrand, "The Many Masks of Anon: Anonymity as Cultural Practice and Reflections in Case Law," *Journal of Technology Law & Policy* 18 (2013), 1. This framework raises the question of whether letters to the editor from ordinary citizens, especially in large city papers, were functionally anonymous despite bearing what appeared to be "real names." In this model, pseudonymity is just partial anonymity. The ability to get more information – to turn the hypothetically

most of the anonymity literature actually discusses pseudonymous speech.

Lee Tien, for example, offers a detailed account of the
uses of "anonymity" online, especially for women, for purposes of explaining why the First Amendment should protect
anonymous speech. But he equates anonymity with the use of
"gender-ambiguous or male names," which is to say, pseudonymity. Tien also argues that the identity of any individual
utterance matters less online because a speaker can become a
listener at any time, and vice versa.[26] This changes the verifi-
ability and believability of anonymous speech. An online
forum collectively, therefore, can offer extra information to
challenge or confirm a particular speaker's credibility.[27] This
"wisdom of crowds" method offers a coherent approach to
factual claims, but has less to say about how artistic or other

    identified speaker into the actually identified speaker – is one measure
    of a given communication's degree of anonymity, as is the recipient's
    motivation to do so. Given the ease with which many supposedly
    "anonymous" speakers can be identified through a bit of technologi-
    cally assisted sleuthing, the name in the newspaper may not be as far
    from the communication identified only by an IP address as some
    assume, as people like David Petraeus and the Harvard sophomore
    recently arrested for making a bomb threat to get out of an exam can
    attest.

[26] He also suggests that "anonymity enables a person to reveal her self
    selectively.... In the context of interactions over time, she can reveal
    progressively more of her self to another, depending on what the
    other person reveals to her." *Ibid.*, 173. But this is very hard with
    anonymity, as opposed to pseudonymity. How do you know it's the
    same person?

[27] Tien, "Who's Afraid of Anonymous Speech? ...," 139, 143.

nonfactual content might be judged. Far from a speaker's identity becoming "less important" in an online community, as Tien argues, her identity can be vital. At the most basic level, a popular pseudonymous author will have a wider platform for her next endeavor. Her identity matters a great deal – it's just not connected to her legal name.

Lyrissa Lidsky and Thomas Cotter also treat pseudonymity as a variant of anonymity in their First Amendment analysis. They suggest that pseudonymity is distinguishable primarily because it has more capacity to deceive about its own status than overt anonymity, because people might not know that James Tiptree, Jr. is a pseudonym for Alice Sheldon. They further note that the person behind a pseudonym may be known to an intermediary (though this is also true with anonymous speech online), and that persistent pseudonyms may develop their own authority over time, as truly anonymous speech does not.[28]

Other legal accounts, such as Laura Heymann's, engage with the meaning of pseudonymity from the perspective of the audience's expectations, including the outrage that occurs when someone claims to represent the authentic perspective of an ethnic or gender identity they don't possess.[29]

---

[28] Lyrissa B. Lidsky & Thomas F. Cotter, "Authorship, Audiences, and Anonymous Speech," *Notre Dame Law Review* 82 (2013), 1537, 1567–1568.

[29] Laura A. Heymann, "The Birth of the Authornym: Authorship, Pseudonymity, and Trademark Law," *Notre Dame Law Review* 80

But neither the "pseudonymity is anonymity over time" or "pseudonymity serves an author-function for audiences" approach spends much time on the specific benefits to speakers of having persistent identities, as opposed to the freedoms speakers can also achieve through anonymity. It's these benefits that interest me, and that are most under threat in a pervasively tracked and re-identified world.

Reading *Lolita* as Lolita: pseudonym cultures

Law isn't everything. The contractual and social regimes under which we operate profoundly shape behavior and identity-play. The story of Google+, Google's Facebook competitor, reveals some of the tensions surrounding pseudonymity. Defenses of pseudonymity against Google's attempts to reject the practice focused, understandably, on the harms that pseudonyms can guard against. But lurking underneath is also a more positive account of the benefits pseudonyms can unlock.

Many people, particularly those who are extremely secure in their identities (especially those who are white, male, and steadily employed), have little sympathy for pseudonymic participation. This lack of understanding was highlighted by the initial deployment of Google+, which demanded "real names." At the same time, Google told users to give the name by which

(2005), 1377, 1446. Greg Lastowka, "The Trademark Function of Authorship," *Boston University Law Revew* 85 (2005), 1171, 1241.

they were "commonly" known to others – which was, for numerous people known in particular communities, actually a pseudonym. (As it happens, pseudonyms are also common on Facebook, but the issue wasn't as sharply presented there because naming practices developed more organically on that site, and because many Facebook pseudonyms are not immediately obvious as such to a casual Western observer.[30])

Google's understanding of authenticity and reality was far from neutral. Lady Gaga was sufficiently famous under that name to escape condemnation, but other longstanding

---

[30] "[C]ountless teens who signed up to Facebook late into the game chose to use pseudonyms or nicknames. What's even more noticeable in my data is that an extremely high percentage of people of color used pseudonyms as compared to the white teens that I interviewed." danah boyd, "'Real Names' Policies Are an Abuse of Power," *Zephoria*, August 4, 2011, available at http://www.zephoria.org/thoughts/archives/2011/08/04/real-names.html. Zeynep Tufekci has written that about 10–20 percent of college students use "some sort of nickname" known to friends on Facebook, and that Facebook relies on "embedded, prolonged, sustained interaction, not the exact name or 'real' name"; names are only tools for embedding people in social networks, and thus accepting and recognizing the name is more important than its presence on formal legal documentation. Zeynep Tufekci, "Don't Suspend Scout Finch, Mr. Schmidt. It's Wrong and It's Bad for Business," *Technosociology* (August 30, 2011), available at http://technosociology.org/?p=530; see also boyd, *It's Complicated*, 45–46 (discussing teens' use of fictitious information on Facebook to provide signals with "insider" meaning; "[t]hese practices allowed them to feel control over their profiles, particularly given how often they told me that it was ridiculous for sites to demand this information").

pseudonyms were not.[31] Nor did Google purport to police ghostwriters – having a publicist manage a celebrity's social media accounts is a kind of impersonation, but Google didn't see it as such even though it purported to generally ban impersonation.[32] Google's real name policy was also unevenly enforced – it was used against people whose names looked unreal, even if they were professionally known by them, but not enforced against someone who chose a pseudonym that fit standard Western naming conventions, such as "Jane Donovan."[33] Google's patchy insistence on government-issued ID when an identity was flagged has new resonance given subsequent voter ID initiatives in the United States –

[31] Doctor Popular, for instance, recounted an experience with Google's requirement that Doctor Popular "use the name that I commonly go by in daily life." Google subsequently rejected newspaper articles and statements from past employers verifying that "Doctor Popular" was the name that the writer used in daily life. Doctor Popular, "Google's Antisocial Behavior," *DocPop* (August 6, 2011), available at http://www.docpop.org/2011/08/googles-antisocial-behavior.

[32] Laura Heymann discusses socially acceptable forms of using other identities and contrasts different legal approaches. Laura A. Heymann, "Naming, Identity, and Trademark Law," *Indiana Law Journal* 86 (2011), 381.

[33] As it happened, it also turned out to be easy to misuse the reporting process to get people suspended for impersonation using an obviously fake proof of identity. Gary Walker recounted the user's ability to get an account suspended by providing a bad fake scan of a driver's license, and then to get the account reinstated using an even worse fake. Gary Walker, "A Firsthand Examination of the Google+ Profile Reporting Process," *Cheaper Than Paper* (August 9, 2011), available at http://gewalker.blogspot.com/2011/08/first hand-examination-of-google-profile.html.

initiatives that have clearly disproportionate effects on women and minorities, who are less likely to have an official identification that reflects the names under which they live.[34]

One reason why Google+'s practices became a flashpoint was that they explicitly rejected persistent pseudonymity, denying that a pseudonym with an established reputation had communicative value and that establishing such an identity through Google+ could be worthwhile, either for individual users or for Google+'s communities. While Google ultimately backed down somewhat,[35] the discourse surrounding "real names" revealed fault lines in popular understandings of online identity and its points of attachment with the names by which our governments, schools, and creditors know us. Despite occasional claims that online anonymity is now too entrenched in our culture to change, it's not

---

[34] Reid Wilson, "Five reasons voter identification bills disproportionately impact women," *Washington Post* (November 5, 2013), available at http://www.washingtonpost.com/blogs/govbeat/wp/2013/11/05/five-reasons-voter-identification-bills-disproportionately-impact-women. Keith Bantelea and Erin O'Brien also found that minority participation was associated with the subsequent adoption of restrictive voter ID laws. Keith G. Bentelea & Erin E. O'Brien, "Jim Crow 2.0? Why States Consider and Adopt Restrictive Voter Access Policies," *Perspectives on Politics* 11 (2013), 1088.

[35] Google+ decided to accept pseudonyms, though it still strongly encourages "real names" and routinely attempts to connect identities across services. Eva Galperin & Jillian C. York, "Victory! Google Surrenders in the Nymwars," *Electronic Frontier Foundation* (October 19, 2011), available at https://www.eff.org/deeplinks/2011/10/victory-google-surrenders-nymwars.

at all settled that pseudonymic participation is standard in online discourse.[36] Thus, one common defense of Google+'s real name policy was that real names put "skin in the game" – the ability to connect people with their online behaviors would deter abusive conduct because speakers wouldn't risk a family member, friend, or potential employer finding their vitriol online.[37] A real name policy would deter online conduct inconsistent with some other role: say, a judge posting biased or self-promotional comments on a news site. Connecting with other people who "seemed" real would also mitigate the tendency to dehumanize others online.

As Lee Tien writes, observing that women's practices of preserving safety by offering false information to male strangers long predate the internet, "Part of the problem with the rhetoric of accountability is its portrayal of anonymity as something abnormal; by contrast, women's experiences show that identity information is routinely concealed in an effort to manage interaction."[38] There are many non-abusive

---

[36] "In the online world, the use of screen names or other online identities to mediate communication is now wholly accepted, as is the idea that an online moniker might well bear no relation to the speaker's 'true' identity." Heymann, *The Birth of the Authornym*, 1412.

[37] Cf. Tien, "Who's Afraid of Anonymous Speech? . . .," 140 (discussing claims that anonymity is bad because of lack of accountability); Richard Posner, *The Economics of Justice,* 234–235 (Cambridge, MA: Harvard University Press, 1983) (arguing that "people conceal facts about themselves in order to mislead others").

[38] Tien, "Who's Afraid of Anonymous Speech? . . .," 169; see also *ibid.,* 172 (citing Carol B. Gardner, "Access Information: Public Lies and

forms of expression that a person might reasonably want to avoid exposing to a family member, friend, or potential employer – including the kind of creative activity that I'll discuss below, which regularly attracts mockery. Of particular relevance for academics, the use of pseudonyms in the education newspaper *The Chronicle of Higher Education* is reportedly higher than in any other newspaper – no surprise given the niche subject matter and the employment anxieties of a largely untenured professoriate.[39]

Boyd also pointed out that the idea of using legal names as a reputational constraint works differently for privileged people. A young minority man who uses gang signs in photos with friends in jest or to fit in can easily be misread by outsiders as a criminal, because of background bias and cultural unfamiliarity: "The assumption ... is that the observer is qualified to actually assess someone's reputation. All too often, and especially with marginalized people, the observer takes someone out of context and judges them inappropriately based on what they get online."[40]

Private Peril," 35 Social Problems 384, 387, 390 (1988) (many women feel that "for a man to know their right name [is] in effect for him to have the ability not just to find them again but somehow to control them"; one woman said, "If they know my real name, it's somehow like they've got me forever").

[39] Sarah Kendzior, "Academia's indentured servants," *Al-Jazeera* (April 11, 2013), http://m.aljazeera.com/story/20134119156459616.

[40] For example, a person may pretend to adhere to his community's norms surrounding gang membership or sexuality, while wishing to dissent and leave; if he uses his real name online, his apparent acquiescence becomes set in stone. boyd, *'Real Names.'*

Moreover, the empirical evidence on real name policies as deterrents of misbehavior is unpromising. Real names (or names presented as real names) don't do much to deter flame wars on Facebook – the disinhibition encouraged by online contact seems to persist regardless.[41] South Korea's "real name" requirement for internet use also doesn't seem to have decreased scurrilous commentary (and was abandoned when hackers stole all that real name information).[42] More generally, someone who *plans* to hurl abuse can also easily plan to use an identity that looks real, but isn't. Serious impersonation – presenting oneself as another recognizable

---

[41] Some research suggests that students who know each other's names are more abusive online, not less, and other research suggests that removing anonymity would have limited effects. Laura Marcus, "Removing anonymity won't stop the online flame wars," *The Guardian* (July 12, 2007), available at http://www.guardian.co.uk/technology/2007/jul/12/guardianweeklytechnologysection.privacy. John Suler explores different causes of disinhibition online, not all related to pseudonymity. John Suler, "The Online Disinhibition Effect," *Cyberpsychology & Behavior* 7 (2004), 321–326.

[42] John Leitner reports no notable decrease in "defamatory" comments after the implementation of a real name identification policy aimed at averting defamation. John Leitner, "Identifying the Problem: Korea's Initial Experience with Mandatory Real Name Verification on Internet Portals," *Journal of Korean Law* 9 (2009), 83. "[In 2011], after a huge security breach, the [South Korean] government said it would abandon the system. Hackers stole 35 million Internet users' national identification numbers, which they had been required to supply when registering on Web sites to verify their identities." Eric Pfanner, "Naming Names on the Internet," *New York Times* (September 4, 2011), available at https://www.nytimes.com/2011/09/05/technology/naming-names-on-the-internet.html?_r=1.

person in order to deceive an audience – isn't the target of real name policies, and is hard to deter in the context of online communication as we now know it. As with political speech, and as in the *Koch Industries* case, it might make more sense to respect the audience's ability to figure out that the "Austin Sarat" commenting intemperately on a blog post may not be Austin Sarat; this is often fairly easy. Instead of focusing on names, online discourse would be better served by comment moderation or other forms of curation that can operate to serve similar purposes as norms of behavior in physical public spaces, where we likewise don't usually know legal names but nonetheless generally expect certain constraints to hold.

Real names nonetheless seemed like a cheap fix because Google didn't recognize their costs. It wasn't accidental that people (mainly men) with the ability to structure technologies didn't notice the beneficial and protective uses of pseudonyms. Often, persistent pseudonyms flew under the radar, as people with non-Western names adopted Western-sounding pseudonyms and didn't contest Facebook's assumption that they were using "real" names.[43] Likewise, "African-American teens who use social media are more likely than white teens to say that they post fake information to their profiles

---

[43] This leaves them at risk of losing their audiences, however. Chinese political blogger Michael Anti lost Facebook access for using a pseudonym. Tini Tran, "Activist Michael Anti Furious He Lost Facebook Account – While Zuckerberg's Dog Has Own Page," *Huffington Post* (March 8, 2011), available at http://www.huffingtonpost.com/2011/03/08/michael-anti-facebook_n_832771.html.

(39% vs. 21%),"[44] though the information might not be obviously fake. All these choices were, in a very real sense, unseen by the relevant decision-makers – but not unaffected. People whose jobs, educational opportunities, physical security, or emotional stability aren't at risk from associating their opinions with their legal names may perceive the risks of association as low for everyone. Not having to know or care about the good reasons why other people might present different identities in different situations is a privilege of power.

Google's initial response to the people who believed that they risked harm from using their legal names, or that they simply deserved to be addressed by the names they routinely used, was unsympathetic. CEO Eric Schmidt declared Google+ optional (despite Google's simultaneous aspiration to migrate everyone using Google services to Google+) and suggested that people who needed pseudonymity, such as political dissidents and battered women, just shouldn't use it. The internet, he contended, would be "better" if we knew that others were real people and not dogs or fakes.[45] Schmidt's reasoning implies that it would be better if people at risk of unwarranted consequences from using their real

---

[44] Mary Madden, Amanda Lenhart, Sandra Cortesi, Urs Gasser, Maeve Duggan, Aaron Smith, & Meredith Beaton, "Teens, Social Media, and Privacy," Pew Research Center (May 21, 2013), available at http://www.pewinternet.org/files/2013/05/PIP_TeensSocialMediaand Privacy_PDF.pdf.

[45] Andy Carvin publically posted Eric Schmidt's words on Google+. Andy Carvin (August 30, 2011), available at https://plus.google.com/+AndyCarvin/posts/CjM2MPKocQP.

names didn't exist, which is true in some sense, but unhelpful. It was also not clear that there were plagues of otherwise undetectable dogs or fake people using the internet. In another context related to free speech, Justice Brandeis coined the phrase "men feared witches and burnt women,"[46] and that caution about imagined harms and missed targets seems particularly relevant where exposure of legal names could have serious practical repercussions – for example, for women who identify as witches but work for evangelical employers.

Researcher danah boyd, whose own name bears small but obvious differences from standard Western naming conventions, quoted numerous people defending pseudonymity, pointing to the particular utility of pseudonyms for women:

> "I am a high school teacher, privacy is of the utmost importance."
>
> "I have used this name/account in a work context, my entire family know this name and my friends know this name. It enables me to participate online without being subject to harassment that at one point in time [led] to my employer having to change their number so that calls could get through."
>
> "I do not feel safe using my real name online as I have had people track me down from my online presence and had coworkers invade my private life."

---

[46] *Whitney v. California*, 274 U.S. 357, 376 (1927) (Brandeis, J., concurring).

"I've been stalked. I'm a rape survivor. I am a government employee that is prohibited from using my IRL [name in real life]."

"As a former victim of stalking that impacted my family I've used [my nickname] online for about 7 years."

"[this name] is a pseudonym I use to protect myself. My web site can be rather controversial and it has been used against me once."

"I started using [this name] to have at least a little layer of anonymity between me and people who act inappropriately/criminally. I think the 'real names' policy hurts women in particular."

"I enjoy being part of a global and open conversation, but I don't wish for my opinions to offend conservative and religious people I know or am related to. Also I don't want my husband's Govt career impacted by his opinionated wife, or for his staff to feel in any way uncomfortable because of my views."

... "This identity was used to protect my real identity as I am gay and my family live in a small village where if it were openly known that their son was gay they would have problems."

"I go by [a] pseudonym for safety reasons. Being female, I am wary of internet harassment."

It's worth emphasizing that many of these repeatedly mentioned concerns – rape, stalking, teaching with its norm of hiding the teacher's personal life from students, government employment – are disproportionately associated with women. Boyd concludes that "[t]he people who most heavily rely on pseudonyms in online spaces are those who are most marginalized by systems of power."[47] Adding insult to injury, requiring a person to use a name that she doesn't want to use can strike at vital elements of her identity, forcing her to acknowledge outside control over a key piece of information that distinguishes her from other people.[48]

As a result of these gendered vulnerabilities, an internet user might wish to be perceived as male, like Sheldon/ Tiptree. A male identity can avoid a lot of hassle, harassment, and abuse online.[49] (One notable recent account comes

[47] boyd, *'Real Names.'* Activists compiled a list of groups that will be disadvantaged by a "real names" policy. Geek Feminism Wiki, "Who is harmed by a 'Real Names' policy?", available at http://geekfemin ism.wikia.com/wiki/Who_is_harmed_by_a_%22Real_Names%22_pol icy. For example, pseudonyms help separate audiences, allowing scientists to speak to colleagues in one venue and to the public in another; they protect against harassment transferring to a blogger's day job; they separate professional lives from writing lives. Maggie Koerth-Baker, "Dispatch from the Nymwars: Pseudonyms and science" (August 22, 2011), available at http://boingboing.net/ 2011/08/22/dispatch-from-the-nymwars-pseudonyms-and-science. html. Heymann specifically discusses mystery novelist Amanda Cross/Columbia professor Carolyn Helibrun, who chose different publishing names to protect her chance at getting tenure. Heymann, *Naming, Identity*, 433.

[48] Heymann discusses control over naming as a coercive power, applied for example to slaves and immigrants. Heymann, *Naming, Identity*, 406.

[49] Danielle Keats Citron, for example, identified this as a defensive measure given the lack of more substantive protections against harassment online. Danielle Keats Citron, "Law's Expressive Value In Combating Cyber Gender Harassment," *Michigan Law*

from a man who adopted a female identity on a dating site for all of two hours before he was demoralized enough by the abuse he received – from men ostensibly sexually interested in women – to quit.)[50] But there are also female-dominated spaces online, and reasons why participants in those spaces may choose pseudonyms, even when direct gender-based flaming and harassment is an unusual problem.

Pseudonymity, in fact, has a wide range of motivations and uses that can't be reduced to a desire to be irresponsible, as Google+ assumed. These functions of pseudonymity are connected to relations that resist commodification and the economic logic of "accountability." People with separate online pseudonyms are disproportionately likely to be using

Review 180 (2009), 373, 387–388. Chat users with female names receive more malicious messages. "Female-Name Chat Users Get 25 Times More Malicious Messages," *Phys Org* (May 9, 2006), available at http://phys.org/news66401288.html. Heymann also relatedly suggests that a pseudonym may be used "to deracialize attribution, to release the text from the burdens of identity and of group membership and allow the text to stand on its own," though it's notable that she doesn't cite examples of the burdens actually lifting (while she cites many examples of culturally appropriative pseudonyms whose perceived identity informed readers' views of the relevant texts). What "allowing the text to stand on its own" reduces to in practice seems to be getting the audience to perceive the speaker as an unmarked member of the dominant groups. Heymann, *Naming, Identity*, 1401.

[50] Rebecca Rose, "Man Poses as Woman on Online Dating Site; Barely Lasts Two Hours," *Jezebel* (January 13, 2014), available at http://jezebel.com/man-poses-as-woman-on-online-dating-site-barely-lasts-1500707724.

the internet for social rather than business reasons. This practice is often divided by class, because many users are not positioned to benefit economically from a web presence under their legal names, and thus embrace the self-expressive and communicative functions of pseudonyms.[51]

Creative media fandom – communities in which people create fan fiction and other new, noncommercial works based on existing books, television shows, movies, and the like – offers many such spaces where people who identify as women (and, more broadly, people who don't identify as straight men) are the default.[52] Media fandom is not a utopia; it's not free of gender policing, much less sexism, racism, or other forms of discrimination. But it also doesn't resemble the online spaces in which merely having a female name generates hostility and rape threats.

In creative media fandom, participation is nonetheless pseudonymous by default.[53] Pseudonymity creates a distinct

---

[51] Emlyn, "Google+, the pseudonym banstick, and the netizen cultural schism," *Point 7* (July 7, 2011), available at https://point7.word press.com/2011/07/24/google-the-pseudonym-banstick-and-the-neti zen-cultural-schism.

[52] Anne Kustritz, "Productive (cyber) public space: Slash fan fiction's multiple imaginary," Doctoral dissertation, University of Michigan (2007).

[53] Fandom pseudonyms fit well into Ekstrand's overlapping categories of beneficial motivations for pseudonymity: following convention; directing focus to the text or the community, rather than to the individual author; safety against potential oppression/negative consequences for speech; a rhetorical strategy to distinguish the persuasiveness of one's arguments from one's identity and to identify

persona that, among other things, can be sexually explicit. "It's one thing for your co-workers, domestic partners, or children to know you're a 'Trekkie,' it's another to know you're a producer of pornography with gay overtones." A fan author may understand her pseudonym as protecting her privacy "for the sake of [her] family," and as dissociating her professional name and publications from her fan identity.[54] Protecting a professional identity is a reasonable concern in a world in which blogging about science, or having private photos disseminated against one's will, can lead to job and physical threats.[55] This is an example of "obscurity by

the speaker with important historical figures or viewpoints; pleasure and the thrill of secrets or of implausibly impersonating a public figure; protection for people disadvantaged by class or gender; preservation of privacy; and spontaneity. Ekstrand, "The Many Masks of Anon ...", 7–22. As with many legal scholars, her analysis doesn't generally distinguish between pseudonymity and anonymity at the level of doctrine, even though she begins by differentiating the two; this grouping may result from her ultimate focus on the case law, which generally does treat pseudonymity as anonymity.

[54] Kylie Lee, "Confronting 'Enterpise' Slash Fan Fiction," *Extrapolation* 44 (2003), 69, 73.

[55] Erica Goode discusses the phenomenon of "revenge porn." Erica Goode, "Victims Push Laws to End Online Revenge Posts," *New York Times* (September 23, 2013). Tara C. Smith recounts threats to employment and safety: "HIV denier Andrew Maniotis showed up, unannounced, at my work office one day a few years ago. The recently-arrested 'David Mabus' showed up at an atheist convention. While using a pseudonym doesn't always protect you – certainly many pseuds have been outed by those willing to do the detective work – it at least offers you some measure of protection from threats, both online and off." Tara C. Smith, "On the value of pseudonyms,"

design": using context-specific identities to preserve privacy even for behavior that is in some sense public, recreating the kind of privacy by default that formerly existed in train stations and other spaces in which strangers gathered.[56]

Writing fan fiction under a pseudonym also provides more general protection from the culturally devalued status of being a media fan, and liberates the fan writer to write: by making her work seem "private" or disconnected from her legal identity even as it's publicly distributed, the pseudonym frees the writer from the expectations surrounding claims to be an "author."[57] Under a pseudonym, a creator doesn't have to take herself seriously when she experiments with styles or topics – or she can take herself seriously while simultaneously using the pseudonym to disavow the full

Science Blogs (August 23, 2011), available at http://scienceblogs.com/aetiology/2011/08/on_the_value_of_pseudonyms.php.

[56] See Jeremy Hainsworth, "Obscurity by Design May Protect Consumers Better Than Privacy by Design, Speaker Says," *Electronic Commerce & Law Report* (February 20, 2014) ("'If an individual is obscure, it means a critical observer is not allowed to make sense of their identity,' [Woodrow Hartzog] said. 'We don't have the key to unlock or make sense of a certain piece of information.'").

[57] "[G]ender imbalance in literary and mass cultural production doesn't just affect venue, opportunity, and reception for active writers; it affects people even wanting to try. It affects people even *claiming* to be trying. Fanfiction has given many writers permission and encouragement to do something they'd never imagined they could do – in part because they can do it in private, without seeming to arrogantly lay claim to the culturally valued and vaunted status of 'writer.'" Anne Jamison, *Fic: Why Fanfiction Is Taking over the World* (Dallas: BenBella Books, 2013), 19–20.

extent of her investment, protecting her self-concept against potential failure. The freedom of anonymity – the freedom associated with confessing one's most intimate secrets to a stranger – can be achieved alongside a persistent connection, if the speaker and her audience so desire.

As Julie Cohen has explained, privacy is a process of boundary management that enables the creation and recreation of the self.[58] Pseudonyms allow this boundary management to take place in public. Pseudonymous members of a community can engage in selective disclosures to other people who are also pseudonymous and thus playing particular versions of themselves; these disclosures can involve highly intimate personal details, but still feel safe because of the distance from a legal identity. This safety then has a generative effect, enabling self-expression and the development of new perspectives and experiences. Pseudonymity's shielding functions can thus be tightly linked to its creative functions.

These multiple affordances illustrate the utility of distinguishing anonymity from persistent pseudonymity, even when we're mostly concerned about diminishing bad behavior. Someone who writes sexually explicit fiction may not want that to be the first thing a next-door neighbor discovers about her. At the same time, she is likely to want her erotica-writing identity to be persistent, so that it can accrue the benefits of reputation, and this will constrain her behavior

---

[58] Julie E. Cohen, "What Privacy Is For," *Harvard Law Review* 126 (2013), 1905.

within the community she's using the identity in. Reputation and legal names are not the same, and efforts directed at the latter attempting to influence the former won't get the desired results.[59]

Even if there were no need for defensive measures, then, pseudonymity would still fulfill important purposes. Like the rapper Rick Ross, fans use pseudonyms as part of a creative purpose. Media fans choose names that announce their fannish interests and allegiances.[60] Many fans use pseudonyms to declare their affiliations (kirklovesspock has a particular

---

[59] Julian Dibbell reports that anonymous, new visitors to a virtual world behaved with fewer constraints than those who made "the critical passage from anonymity to pseudonymity, developing the concern for their character's reputation that marks the attainment of virtual adulthood." Julian Dibbell, *My Tiny Life: Crime and Passion in a Virtual World* (New York: Henry Holt and Co., 1998), 23.

[60] Laura Heymann notes that hackers "take pride in their assumed names," which are "borrowed liberally from the anti-heroes of science fiction, adventure fantasy, and heavy metal rock lyrics, particularly among younger users, and from word plays on technology, nihilism, and violence," and that young people often choose screen names based on "favorite characters, celebrities, or other elements of popular culture." Laura A. Heymann, "A Name I Call Myself: Creativity and Naming," *University of California at Irvine Law Review* 2 (2012), 585, 613. From a different perspective, Marian Merritt found that 1/3 of 7000 adults in 14 countries had used a "fake" online identity and characterized this as "lying." Marian Merritt, "Norton's Cybercrime Report: The Human Impact Reveals Global Cybercrime Epidemic and Our Hidden Hypocrisy," *Norton Community* (September 8, 2010), available at http://community.norton.com/t5/Ask-Marian/Norton-s-Cybercrime-Report-The-Human-Impact-Reveals-Global/ba-p/282432.

take on the Star Trek franchise, and her priorities are probably not the same as those of spockloveskirk) as well as to distinguish their online presences as fans from their presences under their legal names.[61] A fannish name signals membership in fannish groups and suggests that the user won't share in the general cultural devaluation of fandom, even if kirklovesspock finds kirklovesmccoy's opinions misguided.

Are you nobody too? Pseudonyms and communities

Lee Tien notes the potential for pleasure and play in anonymity (that is, pseudonymity), characterizing online pseudonyms as a kind of masquerade ball.[62] While identity-play often seems to risk solipsism, the analogy of the masquerade ball points to the role of pseudonymity in community building. The masquerade gains meaning in the group and the group's reactions over time. Unlike a disguise worn for reasons entirely of one's own, the masquerade assists in the formation of a group identity as well as an individual one. Because building reputational capital requires not just a persistent identity but a persistent community, forming an identity depends on the audience, not just the individual.[63]

---

[61] "Plenty of people who would never dream of dressing up as Princess Leia or as a Klingon at a fan convention were drawn to create online personae that were themselves a kind of fiction." Jamison, *Fic*, 112.

[62] Tien, "Who's Afraid of Anonymous Speech? . . .," 182–183.

[63] See Erving Goffman, *The Presentation of Self in Everyday Life* (Garden City, NY: Doubleday, 1959), 82 (discussing the importance

Pseudonymity supports communities in many ways. It reduces the tension created by pure anonymity, which is generally unpleasant for recipients (at least those who weren't looking for anonymous contact), by reassuring users that they're interacting with specific other people whose identities persist over time.[64] Where, as in the fan communities I discuss here, communities of practice have grown up around pseudonyms, even people otherwise willing to use their legal names may choose pseudonyms, just to fit in.[65] And the pseudonymous norm is enforced *against* other community members: people who publicly connect a fan's pseudonym with her legal or "wallet" name face social sanctions from other fans.[66] The audience thus collaborates in the fan's production of a separate identity, knowing that the fan has another identity that is primary in different contexts but fighting attempts to collapse the two.[67] Though fans can't actually prevent such outings, they can raise the costs of doing so for other community members who are the most

of "teams" working in concert to manage identities and self-presentation).

[64] Stephen A. Rains & Craig R. Scott, "To Identify or Not To Identify: A Theoretical Model of Receiver Responses to Anonymous Communication," *Communication Theory* 17 (2007), 64.

[65] Geek Feminism Wiki, *Who is Harmed*.

[66] Kristina Busse & Karen Hellekson. "Identity, Ethics, and Fan Privacy," in *Fan Culture: Theory/Practice*, eds. Katherine Larsen & Lynn Zubernis (Newcastle: Cambridge Scholars Publishing, 2012), 38.

[67] Cf. Goffman, *The Presentation of Self ...*, 49 (discussing audience collaboration in the maintenance of a particular self-presentation).

likely to have a motive to make the pseudonym-legal name link (usually as the result of some falling out).

The web commenting service Disqus, which allows websites to run comment sections, analyzed its database of hundreds of millions of comments, and concluded that "pseudonyms drive communities." They are often used because they are better than legal names for the purpose at hand: expression and representation of the self to a particular community. Pseudonyms "leave behind personal ties (e.g. job, relationships, privacy) without sacrificing personality." Disqus concluded that pseudonyms were the most valuable contributors to communities, based on its measures of volume and quality. Pseudonymous users contributed 61% of total comments, commenting 6.5 times more frequently than anonymous users and 4.7 times more frequently than Facebook users nominally using "real" names. Moreover, pseudonymous comments were "liked" and replied to more often than comments from anonymous or Facebook commenters, which indicated that these comments supported engagement and interaction.[68] The numbers from the blogs Disqus tracked suggest that fannish communities are examples, not exceptions. People

---

[68] Disqus, "Pseudonyms Drive Communities," accessed January 12, 2014, available at http://disqus.com/research/pseudonyms. Disqus labeled 61% of pseudonym interactions as positive, with 11% negative (flagged for abuse, marked as spam, or deleted), while 34% of anonymous interactions were positive and 11% neutral, and 51% of Facebook interactions were positive and 9% negative; the balance were marked neutral.

who adopt yarn-related pseudonyms on knitting sites are doing something similar, if less culturally fraught.

Thus, the discourse of threat and risk that understandably begins most defenses of pseudonyms online isn't the whole picture. Welcome, comfort, and community can also be found in pseudonyms. A recent cartoon by Jeff Wysaski begins by announcing "we all wear masks," and proceeds to show us four people: "Shannon pretends she's happy; Kevin pretends he's over her; Jake pretends he's confident; Patrick pretends he's Batman."[69] There is joy as well as incongruity in Patrick's choice.

Like Wysaski and his creation Patrick, media fans readily understand that the celebrity Daniel Radcliffe and a poster on the journaling site Tumblr using the name "Daniel Radcliffe" are unlikely to be the same person or have the same interests.[70] Indeed, fans sometimes use pseudonyms for explicit role-playing purposes: pretending to be a favorite character or celebrity (depending on whether the role-play involves fictional characters or "real" people).[71] Role-play is a version of biographical fiction, but its interactivity and newness may seem

---

[69] Jeff Wysaski, "We All Wear Masks," *Pleated Jeans* (December 30, 2013), available at http://www.pleated-jeans.com/2013/12/30/we-all-wear-masks.

[70] Cf. boyd, *It's Complicated*, 46 (noting that teens who provide untrue information on Facebook know that most people who see the information will know the truth).

[71] "Fandom RPGs online are a combination of collaborative fan fiction and traditional role-playing games, in which players write posts, messages, or comments as (or about) characters from established

to present distinct issues from traditional fiction. Scenarios can be minimally changed – the characters from *Sherlock Holmes* all discover and participate in a particular social media site, while also conducting their ordinary activities – or they can be completely different – members of the band Fall Out Boy write diary entries describing their struggle for survival in a post-apocalyptic dystopia. Often such narratives explore sexuality and romance, using familiar characters to gain new perspectives. Within fandom communities, these representations appear as just another kind of pseudonym that supports creative play, not as impersonations designed to be believed. Role-play is thus a bit Yes Men and a bit Rick Ross: playful, but sometimes with a more serious message.

Role-play as a recognizable character or personality has continuities with the phenomenon of men who pretend to be women, or who operate female avatars, in online gaming.[72]

fictional worlds. In some RPGs, players create journals on LiveJournal or other journaling sites as their characters, and write as if their characters were actually users of a journaling service." "Fandom RPG," *Fanlore.Org*, accessed January 12, 2014, available at http://fanlore.org/wiki/Fandom_RPG. The related concept of "RPF" is widely used to describe fiction written about celebrities by people who aren't pretending to be those celebrities but who are likely to be using pseudonyms. "RPF," *Fanlore.Org*, accessed January 12, 2014, available at http://fanlore.org/wiki/RPF. Role-play is a more collaborative activity than writing RPF, because it generally requires multiple people, each pretending to be a particular character or characters.

[72] F. Gregory Lastowka & Dan Hunter, "The Laws of the Virtual Worlds," *California Law Review* 92 (2004), 1, 66–67.; Max Burns, "The Power of Real-World Gender Roles in Second Life,"

Given the pervasiveness of patriarchy and sexualized threats, a woman pretending to be a man requires little explanation; observers have therefore spent more time explaining why men might take on degraded female identities. The motives here are generally understood to be much more hedonistic than practical or self-protective. Such male-identified players are experimenting with transgression of boundaries, which frees them from certain constraints on behavior even as it imposes others.

Role-playing doesn't offer the protection that women sometimes seek from identification as women (everyone likely to see the role-play understands that it's not a "true" identity), any more than other fandom pseudonyms do. Instead, assuming the identity of a particular character provides the boundary-crossing pleasures usually attributed to men with generic female avatars, with the additional benefits of feedback from a preexisting audience with expectations for what counts as a "good" performance of that specific character. Online, a role-player can strive to inhabit her Harry Potter as Daniel Radcliffe did in the movies, or she can strive to inhabit the public persona of Daniel Radcliffe (as he'd react to a zombie uprising, perhaps). The possibilities are limited only by the players' imaginations and the audience's interest.

The pleasure of assuming a different social identity, through role-play or otherwise, can be intense, and it is this

PixelsAndPolicy (November 2, 2009), available at http://www.pixel sandpolicy.com/pixels_and_policy/2009/11/female-avatars.html.

pleasure that has largely gone unremarked in the existing
literature and case law on anonymity/pseudonymity.[73]
Similarly, pseudonymity is a way to disclose personal information or opinions – which in itself can be extremely
rewarding[74] – with less perceived exposure, a way to have
one's cake in public while not being seen to eat it. These are the
kinds of utilities that law often ignores in the service of well-
defined, serious causes of action. For example, Lisa Ramsey
argues that deliberate impersonation of a well-known brand or
person on social networks should be treated as a violation of
trademark law.[75] It's unsurprising that law finds pleasure

[73] Cf. Ekstrand, 35 ("While many of our motivations for acting anonymously are the same [online and offline], there is increased emphasis
on gamesmanship and spontaneity online that courts have yet to
address. Some of that gamesmanship and spontaneity may contain
political speech undertones worthy of First Amendment protection.").

[74] Diana Tamir & Jason P. Mitchell, "Disclosing Information About the
Self is Intrinsically Rewarding," *Proceedings of the National
Academy of Sciences* 109 (2012), 8038, 8041 n 21.

[75] Ramsey, *Brandjacking*, 859. Ramsey's proposal slices a bit finely,
because she identifies disturbing instances of impersonation (such
as a Nine West impersonator who succeeded in getting many women
to send pictures of their bare feet, *ibid.*, 854) as impetus for her
proposal, then attempts to carve out a space for free speech where
a speaker isn't selling anything and the confusion is only over
whether a trademark owner authorized the speaker to use its
mark. *Ibid.*, 859. It's not clear to me that this configuration would
solve the foot fetishist problem. She also suggests that the "real
name" culture on Facebook and Twitter distinguishes those sites
from sites like Livejournal, where pseudonyms are common and
therefore impersonation is less likely to cause harm, *ibid.*, 856,
863; yet as danah boyd has explained, Facebook pseudonyms are

rather embarrassing, and hard to value as against other objectives (truth, avoiding defamation, and so on), but it's still important to discuss both the positive and the defensive sides of pseudonymity, so that we can move beyond the binary of "if you've got nothing to hide, you've got nothing to fear."

Laura Heymann has devoted much attention to the complexities of naming and pseudonymity in law, invoking trademark principles to guide her analysis. Her thesis is that persistent identities should be understood as benefits for *audiences*, just as a trademark benefits consumers by enabling them to identify desired products even if they don't know anything else about the producer, even its legal name. Heymann argues that audiences for creative works (including for an entertaining presentation of a self) have a substantial interest in having some identifier of authorship, but no particular interest in having that identifier match up with any legal name. Mark Twain and Samuel Clemens are, ex ante, equivalent to each other and to John Grisham. When interactions are wholly textual, the letters that form the name just don't matter. What audiences care about is what the identified person says, and the reputation that becomes attached to the identity.[76]

Yet audience interests in attributing work to a stable identity, like the concept of defense from negative consequences,

also quite common (if less visible as such), and parody Twitter accounts are legion. danah boyd, *'Real Names.'*

[76] Heymann, *The Birth of the Authornym*, 1396–1397; see also Post, supra (distinguishing anonymity from pseudonymity because of ability to build up reputational capital over time).

can't explain everything that's going on with pseudonyms, especially once they're detached from looking like standard names that might appear on American driver's licenses. Rick Ross is not the same kind of pseudonym as Samuel Clemens; its choice situates the rapper in a particular way in his artistic community. Samlicker81, the pseudonym of a fan character on the cult TV show *Supernatural*, isn't the same kind of name as Mark Twain. The audience learns something much more specific about the character Becky Rosen when it learns that she chose to identify herself to other fans as someone interested in licking Sam Winchester (and probably as someone born in 1981, though that's less clearly entailed by the name). Sam is one of the two main characters, and she has thus signaled her favorite character and some sort of erotically charged feeling – serious or humorous or both – for him.[77] Within the narrative and the meta-narrative, her fellow fans understand which Sam she wanted to lick because she's part of the *Supernatural* fan community, where there's only one Sam of note. Indeed, an actual fan of the TV show *Supernatural* later adopted Becky Rosen's pseudonym and posted fiction as samlicker81. The fan's choice of this particular pseudonym let her talk back to, and play along with, the show's creators/corporate copyright owners; she was reasserting fans' own ability to present themselves despite their largely negative portrayals in mainstream

---

[77] Heymann writes that a pseudonym can "signal a particular textual interpretation to readers. *Ibid.*, 1406.

media like *Supernatural*.[78] Because of this creative inter-
change, pseudonyms in online communities aren't just
addresses to an audience that receives messages. Instead, the
communities constitute like-minded souls and quite likely
equal participants in dialogue and feedback. Pseudonyms rein-
force each other, creating individuals within the crowd.

Like revolutionary cells – specifically, like the Founding
Fathers taking on names derived from antiquity to signal a
common commitment to classical ideals in the *Federalist
Papers* – media fans adopt identities that define and distinguish them, though often only to those in the know.
Understanding pseudonymity becomes a competence worth
having, a marker of belonging. It's this communitarian, associative aspect that has been least acknowledged in much of
the legal literature addressing pseudonymity. While anonymity isolates people from each other, or dissolves them
into an undifferentiated crowd, pseudonymity has the potential to do exactly the opposite.

IV I am somebody . . . else: supporting identity-play

In First Amendment discourse, the defensive role of anonymity and pseudonymity has had pride of place: most cases are
about whether it's legitimate to force someone to expose her
legal name, given the risks she might run in doing so. But the

---

[78] Jamison, *Fic*, 313. When a user chooses the AOL screen name
"boysrch," likewise, some people will infer that he's sexually interested in men. *McVeigh v. Cohen*, 983 F.Supp. 215 (D.D.C. 1998).

trademark and right of publicity cases also have something to tell us about the freedoms conferred by pseudonymity: the expressive and associative functions of a new name. The rapper Rick Ross and the writer James Tiptree, Jr. have hundreds of thousands of online counterparts. Separated, persistent identities are a way for people to create themselves, and to create new works of art, taking advantage of the power that comes from being unseen or partially seen.

A final lesson from online behaviors surrounding pseudonymity is that, in some sense, many people refuse to recognize the possibility of a world without privacy.[79] At the very least, it seems as if citizens online are engaging in a kind of reasoning familiar to students of fetishism: I know very well that I'm not truly anonymous (and not truly Fox Mulder's vampire wife), but all the same ...[80] Denial is not necessarily

---

[79] See Jack M. Balkin, "Old School/New School Speech Regulation," *Harvard Law Review* (forthcoming 2014), available at http://papers. ssrn.com/sol3/papers.cfm?abstract_id=2377526, manuscript, 60 ("In a world of pervasive surveillance, the state and owners of private infrastructure may not want to achieve chilling effects with respect to most people; instead, they may want most people just to chill out").

[80] Octave Mannoni, "Je sais bien, mais quand-même ..." *Clefs pour l'imaginaire ou l'autre scène* (Paris: Editions du Seuil, 1969), 9–33. "Many fans labor in a space they perceive as closed, with little idea of how many lurkers are reading but not engaging ... [F]ans are certainly not members of the only subculture that exists in semipublic spaces and nevertheless expects outside observers to respectfully and conscientiously abide by their internal rules." Busse & Hellekson, "Identity, Ethics, and Fan Privacy," in *Fan Culture: Theory / Practice*, 46–47.

pathological. In a surveillance state it might be a tool for psychological survival, a way of claiming some remnants of power. Thus, although my focus has been on uses of pseudonymity that generally only affect relations between individuals rather than protecting them from their governments or their corporate overlords, I think there are connections with the other contributions in this volume. Against the odds, even against rationality, we continue to make ourselves and we continue to make art. That might not be enough, but it's something.

3

Enough About Me: Why Privacy is About Power, not Consent (or Harm)

Lisa M. Austin

Introduction

If privacy is supposedly dead, it is a death whose report has been greatly exaggerated. The ongoing Snowden revelations have made us all acutely aware that the internet has become an infrastructure of surveillance. And yet the global push back against surveillance shows that at least the value of privacy is very much alive and well, even if its practice has taken a beating. Much of this reaction has focused on the role of national security agencies, primarily the US NSA, in undermining internet privacy and freedom. Discussions center on law reform, including substantive statutory changes, the overturning of problematic constitutional doctrines, and improved oversight. A broader discussion regarding lawful access by law enforcement agencies and their information sharing practices both with each other, with national security agencies, and across borders, also is necessary. However, no state authority created this infrastructure of surveillance. As Bruce Schneier recently stated, "The NSA didn't build its eavesdropping system from scratch; it got itself a copy of what the corporate world was already collecting ... Surveillance is the business model of the Internet."[1] If we want to revive privacy from its current death throes, attending to the activities of state authorities is not enough. We need to understand the business model of surveillance and the role of law in enabling both it and the corporate–state nexus.

The easiest thing to do would be to point to the weak private-sector privacy law in the United States, as compared with other jurisdictions such as Canada or Europe, which both have broad privacy protection modeled on Fair Information Practices (FIPs). Prior to the Snowden revelations there were important US initiatives along these lines, which look all the more important in the current context.[2] This model is often characterized in terms of informational self-determination, or the ability of individuals to have

---

[1] Bruce Schneier, "'Stalker economy' here to stay" *CNN* (November 26, 2013), accessed March 5, 2014, available at http://edition.cnn.com/2013/11/20/opinion/schneier-stalker-economy/index.html.

[2] Federal Trade Commissioner, "Protecting Consumer Privacy in an Era of Rapid Change" (2012); The White House, "Consumer Data Privacy in a Networked World: A Framework for Protecting Privacy and Promoting Innovation in the Global Digital Economy" (2012).

control over the collection, use, and disclosure of their personal information.[3] Given the strong role that consent plays in these regimes, in this chapter I label this the consent-based model of privacy protection.

Although there are many practical, cognitive, and theoretical problems with an individual-consent model, the problems I outline are structural. These structural issues fall into two main categories. First, the individual-consent model was originally developed to deal with the relationship between an individual and an organization, as distinct from either relationships between individuals within the general social sphere or relationships between individuals and the state in the traditional law enforcement context. However, as outlined below, contemporary internet companies operate as information intermediaries, mediating all of these various relationships, often in complex ways. Second, implementing a consent-based regime, through legislation and adjudication under that legislation, requires that we move beyond a subjective account of privacy, where the individual decides in relation to his or her own information, to a more objective account of privacy that can address both countervailing interests arising out of multiple relationships and the questions regarding what type and form of consent is required (opt-in, opt-out, implied, explicit). Both of these structural issues point to the importance of non-consent-based ideas of privacy. The

---

[3] This phrase comes from the population census decision of the German Federal Constitutional Court: BVerfGE 65, 1 (1983).

problem that this generates, however, is that the traditional accounts of privacy ready at hand are usually based upon general social norms, ideas of intrusion into protected spheres with an emphasis on private places, or confidential and sensitive information. Many have critiqued such accounts as inadequate in the face of contemporary information practices, offering an unduly constrained understanding of privacy.[4]

To show how these structural problems can work to enable surveillance, I outline two examples from the Canadian experience that highlight a range of concerns regarding internet surveillance: social media and lawful access. Utilizing these cautionary tales, I argue that the structural defects associated with the consent model operate to undermine privacy and facilitate surveillance.

The alternative I propose is to focus on power. This has two components, which take two different lessons from our ideas of trespass. The first is that constitutional ideas of search and seizure have their roots in trespass law, but the significance of this is not property but the rule of law. The rule of law has been traditionally concerned with constraining power and its values are an important source of ideas in relation to surveillance. I call this the "power-over" analysis.

---

[4] Helen Nissenbaum, "Protecting Privacy in an Information Age: The Problem of Privacy in Public," *Law and Philosophy* 17 (1998), 559; Lisa Austin, "Privacy and the Question of Technology," *Law and Philosophy* 22 (2003), 119; Julie Cohen, "Privacy, Visibility, Transparency, and Exposure," *University of Chicago Law Review* 75 (2008), 181.

The second lesson is that trespass liability is not about redressing harms but about protecting the control powers of owners. Legal powers are about the facilitative dimensions of law, where law empowers us do things that we otherwise would not be able to do. I call this the "power-to" analysis. It can help us move beyond a search for privacy harms and look to law's role in providing some of the basic conditions for social interaction. Taken together, I argue that these ideas can provide us with an important set of ideas for responding to contemporary surveillance.

Although these twin ideas of power share an affinity with many existing models of privacy, they also shift the emphasis in privacy law away from *privacy* and towards *law*. We need to enlarge our focus and connect these important debates of the information age with debates about the nature of law.

Consent and its discontents

As Julie Cohen has recently noted, despite the differences between European and US traditions regarding privacy, "there has been increasing convergence around the importance of consent as a standard for assessing compliance with legal obligations to protect personal information."[5] The US context for private-sector privacy regulation has tended to rely on notice-and-choice and self-regulatory models. The

[5] Julie Cohen, "Between Truth and Power," in *Freedom and Property of Information: The Philosophy of Law Meets the Philosophy of Technology*, eds. Mireille Hildebrandt & Bibi van den Berg (Routledge, 2014).

European Data Directive, and the state legislation that implements it, is modeled on the more robust set of Fair Information Practices (FIPs).[6] These include the principle of collection limitation, which requires knowledge and consent where appropriate, but also the principles of data quality, purpose specification, use limitation, security safeguards, openness, individual participation, and accountability. Canada's private-sector model is somewhat in-between. The *Personal Information Protection and Electronic Documents Act* (PIPEDA) adopts the Canadian Standards Association Model Code for the Protection of Personal Information, which was a voluntary industry standard but one modeled on FIPs.[7] Consent is seen as one of the cornerstones of the Act.

This growing international consensus regarding the importance of individual control and consent in relation to personal information comes at a time of growing anxiety regarding the limits of consent, including serious concerns regarding cognitive limits to providing meaningful consent.[8]

---

[6] See, for example, OECD, "Guidelines on the Protection of Privacy and Transborder Flows of Personal Data, Annex to Recommendation of the Council" (23 September 1980); Directive (EC) of the European Parliament and of the Council of 24 October 1995 on the protection of individuals with regard to the processing of personal data and on the free movement of such data [1995] OJ L281/31.

[7] Personal Information Protection and Electronic Documents Act, S.C. 2000, c.5; CAN/CSA-Q830–96. [PIPEDA]

[8] Alessandro Acquisti & Jens Grossklags, "What Can Behavioral Economics Teach Us About Privacy?" in *Digital Privacy: Theory, Technologies and Practices*, eds. Alessandro Acquisti, Sabrina De Capitani di Vimercati, Stefanos Gritzalis, & Costas

As Kevin Haggerty argues, the operation of consent in practice is "perhaps the biggest charade in privacy law," enabling rather than constraining collection.[9] Another set of concerns focus on the normative deficiencies of a consent model.[10] I agree with much of this debate but want to instead focus here on the serious *structural* problems associated with consent.

Before outlining what I consider to be the structural problems associated with consent-based models of privacy protection, it is important to note a related structural problem relating to *what* consent regulates. This model of privacy law regulates personal information, which includes information about an "identifiable" person.[11] The problem is that this

Lambrinoudakis (Auerbach Publications, 2007); Daniel Solove, "Privacy Self-Management and the Consent Dilemma," *Harvard Law Review* 126 (2013); Fred H. Cate, "The Failure of Fair Information Practices Principles," in *Consumer Protection in the Age of the Information Economy*, ed. Jane K. Winn (Burlington: Ashgate, 2006) 360.

[9] Kevin D. Haggerty, "What's wrong with privacy protections? Provocations from a fifth columnist," Chapter 4 of this volume.

[10] For an outline of these see Lisa M. Austin, "Is Consent the Foundation of Fair Information Practices: Canada's Experience under PIPEDA," *University of Toronto Law Journal* 56 (2006), 181.

[11] Lisa M. Austin, "Reviewing PIPEDA: Control, Privacy and the Limits of Fair Information Practices," *Canadian Business Law Journal* 44 (2006), 21; Paul Ohm, "Broken Promises of Privacy: Responding to the Surprising Failure of Anonymization" *UCLA Law Review* 57 (2010), 1701; Paul M. Schwartz & Daniel J. Solove, "The PII Problem: Privacy and a New Concept of Personally Identifiable Information," *New York University Law Review* 86 (2011), 1814. Note that many American statutes refer to "personally identifiable information" (PII) whereas Canadian statutes refer to "personal

is an all-or-nothing model where FIPs apply in relation to the collection, use, and disclosure of personal information but not other forms: information that is de-identified is still at risk of re-identification and the nature of this risk varies. If the risk of re-identification lies along a spectrum then a regulatory model based on a binary determination of "identifiable or not" is problematic. However, in this chapter I want to set this aside and focus on consent.

The first type of structural problem associated with consent concerns the relationship that is supposed to be regulated through this consent-based model. The basic framework of fair information practices was developed to address the issue of the collection, use, and disclosure of personal information by large organizations in the context of concerns regarding computer networks.[12] The key relationship informing this privacy model is the individual–organization relationship. However, contemporary internet companies increasingly operate as information intermediaries, where their practices mediate other types of relationships in complex ways. This raises a number of questions regarding how a regime modeled on one type of relationship can regulate practices that in fact cover multiple, often intersecting, relationships.

Robert Post's work can highlight the problem. As he helpfully shows, there are multiple important spheres of life with

information" but then define this to include information about an "identifiable" individual.

[12] See OECD Guidelines.

different key relationships that help to define their characteristic privacy norms. One is the sphere of social life, governed by norms of civility. Another is the public sphere,
where the "public" is constructed and maintained through
mass media, and is governed by norms of public accountability. According to Post, these can be in deep tension with one
another and both can be displaced by the "the claims of the
state to control and regulate communal life," including
through state search powers.[13] All of these are different
again from the ideas of privacy that animate the practices
of large organizations and their relationships with individuals, which Post suggests "are not sufficiently textured or
dense to sustain vital rules of civility" and thus do not reflect
the "social and communal character" of privacy.[14]

Many have written about the deeply contextual nature of
privacy.[15] What we also need to keep in view is the key
differences in context that characteristically shape different
legal models of privacy protection. The basic relationships at
issue in tort law differ from those in data protection law,
which differ again from those at issue in constitutional law.
But information intermediaries operate within a complex of
multiple relationships that intersect with all of these. As

[13] Robert C. Post, "The Social Foundations of Privacy: Community and
Self in the Common Law Tort," *California Law Review* 77 (1989): 1010.
[14] *Ibid.*, 1009.
[15] Helen Nissenbaum, "Privacy as Contextual Integrity," *Washington
Law Review* 79 (2004), 119; Daniel J. Solove, "A Taxonomy of
Privacy," *University of Pennsylvania Law Review* 154 (2006), 477.

organizations, they collect, use, and disclose information about their clients and so fall within the organizational logic addressed by fair information practices. Many also play a unique role within modern communications by providing the tools and platforms that facilitate social interactions. They therefore help to constitute the sphere of social life within which we interact with each other; they also have business interests that are intrinsically tied to these interactions. Similarly, many social media sites play a role in constituting the "public," although quite differently than the forms of mass media that Post wrote about. Finally, these companies act as intermediaries between individuals and the state, complying with various types of requests and orders by state authorities for information about their clients. In all these ways, information intermediaries are enmeshed within a variety of relationships that have been traditionally characterized by very different, and at times incompatible, norms.

There are therefore important questions to ask when the information practices of an organization go beyond the direct relationship that the organization has with an individual and impacts on other relationships. We should not think that simply applying a consent model, or for that matter any of the other fair information principles developed more than thirty years ago, will suffice.

The response to this criticism of the potential anemia of the consent model is this: notwithstanding the limited context in which it developed, consent is just a better way to think about privacy in general, much better than what we have developed in relation to tort law and constitutional law, and so we should actually feel more optimistic regarding its ability to deal with the reality of information intermediaries than other ideas of privacy. Those other ideas of privacy have focused on regulating "private" information rather than "personal information." This leads them to repeatedly fall back on ideas of privacy that tie it to intimate, confidential, or sensitive information, or a narrow view of the private sphere as distinguished from the public. If we instead focus on "personal information" then we regulate a much broader set of data and we leave it up to individuals to determine for themselves what they want to share, with whom, and on what terms.

This is an initially attractive view. However, in response I want to raise a second set of structural concerns that have to do with how a consent-based privacy regime is implemented. The appeal of individual consent is that it reflects a very individual and subjective understanding of privacy – it is up to me to decide what information about me I want to share and with whom. The problem is that when we create law based on this, we come up against two pressures. One concerns the role of countervailing interests and the other concerns the obligations of the parties who are required to seek consent.

First, consent overprotects privacy because sometimes privacy must yield to other interests in some contexts. This is why we see exceptions to consent in consent-based legislative models that outline a variety of situations that reflect countervailing interests, such as disclosure to the state without consent for law enforcement purposes. To allow individuals control over their personal information in such contexts would overprotect privacy in relation to these other interests.

The further question that this raises is whether, once we accept these as exceptions to consent, we are also accepting that privacy no longer plays a role in interpreting or assessing these exceptions. If individual control over information is the operative understanding of privacy then this would be a reasonable assumption, for an exception to consent then looks like an exception to privacy. However, sometimes the accommodation of countervailing interests is the very place in which the consent model intersects with other privacy models, with their own developed privacy norms. The law enforcement example illustrates this. The classic context of state search and seizure is always one where the state seeks to gain access to information against the wishes of the particular individual targeted. The terms of this access are determined through an analysis framed in terms of a reasonable expectation of privacy, not individual consent. This individual–state relationship then intersects with the organizational logic of FIPs because it is the organization that is tasked with complying with the law enforcement request. Depending on the circumstances, this compliance can be discretionary. The question then centers on what concerns the organization should consider when exercising this discretion. The individual's privacy interest in relation to the state should be one of those concerns, but something more than an idea of individual consent is needed to address this.

The second structural problem with a consent-based regime is that it has to impose obligations on other people to obtain consent, and once it does this there is tremendous pressure to move away from the subjectivity of individual consent to a more objective determination concerning both the privacy interests associated with the information at issue and even the needs of the organizations in their informational practices. For example, organizations need to know what type and form of consent is required (opt-in vs. opt-out, implicit vs. explicit) and they need to know this in advance of seeking any particular individual's privacy preference through consent. These choices usually turn on more objective understandings of how "sensitive" the information is.[16] The legitimate needs of organizations also factor into the question of whether consent should be explicit or can be implied. For example, where the collection of information is seen as necessary to provide a particular service, and notice of that collection is provided, then it does not make a lot of sense to say that an individual can consent to the service but decline consent to the information collection necessarily associated with it. In previous work I outline

[16] This is true of Canada's PIPEDA. One can also see this in the FTC proposals, where "sensitive data" is thought to require explicit opt-in consent in circumstances that would otherwise fit within "commonly accepted practices" (47).

how the idea of "reasonableness," which often involves balancing some of these more objective understandings of privacy against organizational interests, is the real work-horse of this type of legislation and often drives findings of implied consent.[17]

This last point is one of the reasons why this model of privacy protection will not be of much help in curbing the collection of the metadata associated with our online lives which, thanks to the Snowden revelations, has become part of our public debate regarding privacy. Much of what we do now generates digital trails of various kinds. It makes no sense to talk about requiring individuals to consent to the collection of metadata where this is necessarily gener-ated through the provision of a service the individual has consented to. We can debate whether the service can and should be provided in a manner that does not produce such digital by-products, but that is not a question that consent addresses.

These structural defects bring us full circle back to the problem to which a consent-based model of privacy looked so promising a solution. Privacy as individual control over per-sonal information allows individuals to decide for themselves what their privacy preferences are. It is a promising basis for understanding privacy in the context of information and communications technology, where more traditional ideas

---

[17] Austin, "Is Consent the Foundation of Fair Information Practices?"

of a public–private divide, existing general social norms, or a strong emphasis on confidential and sensitive information seem misplaced. And yet consent proves rather anemic, in need of revitalizing through other, more objective, ideas of privacy and their relationship with various countervailing values. The ideas of privacy that are easy to fall back on are the very ones that seem so limited in the context of contemporary threats to privacy, or are those developed within very specific types of relationships that cannot capture the full complexity of privacy and the role played by information intermediaries.

Some cautionary tales

What follows are several cautionary tales about the consent model drawn from the Canadian experience. They illustrate how a consent model, along with its characteristic structural defects, fails to resist pervasive internet surveillance and in some instances even facilitates it.

In order to understand these structural defects it is important to note two important features of the Canadian legal context, which might be thought to temper some of the weaknesses of a consent model. The first is that, under PIPEDA, the collection, use, or disclosure of personal information can be prohibited even when an individual consents. Section 5(3) of PIPEDA provides that "[a]n organization may collect, use or disclose personal information only for purposes that a reasonable person would consider are appropriate in the circumstances." This was added in response to privacy advocates who wanted to require organizations to justify their purposes.[18] The second, which is important to discussions of the corporate–state nexus, is that Canadian constitutional jurisprudence has long rejected the controversial third-party doctrine of US Fourth Amendment law. That an individual has voluntarily shared information with a third party does not mean she has no reasonable expectation of privacy in relation to that information vis-à-vis the state; that the third party voluntarily shares that information with the state does not absolve the state of its constitutional obligation to seek a warrant in appropriate circumstances.[19] The Canadian consent model is therefore situated within a legal context with features that would seem to mitigate some of the defects of a more pure consent model. Nonetheless, it suffers from some notable defects.

Social Media

Facebook provides a good illustration of many of the elements of new internet businesses. First, like other examples of social media, much of the content on Facebook is user-generated.

[18] Stephanie Perrin, Heather H. Black, David H. Flaherty, & T. Murray Rankin, *The Personal Information Protection and Electronic Documents Act: An Annotated Guide* (Toronto: Irwin Law, 2001), 61.

[19] *Smith v. Maryland*, 442 U.S. 735 (1979). This case was rejected in a trilogy of Supreme Court of Canada decisions: *R. v. Duarte*, 1 S.C.R. 30 (1990); *R. v. Wong*, 3 S.C.R. 36 (190); and *R. v. Wise*, 1 S.C.R. 527 (1992).

Facebook claims to have 1.23 billion active monthly users, and 757 million daily active users.[20] Second, much of the revenue for Facebook comes from advertising targeted at these users. Facebook is able to analyze this wealth of information provided by its users and use it to provide "ads that are relevant, engaging and have social context."[21] In the third quarter of 2013, Facebook reported advertisement revenue of US\$ 1.8 billion, representing 89% of its revenue for that period.[22]

In 2008 the Canadian Internet Policy and Public Interest Clinic (CIPPIC) filed a complaint against Facebook with the Office of the Privacy Commissioner of Canada, alleging that a number of Facebook's practices violated PIPEDA. The resulting Report of Findings exhibits many of the tensions that arise due to the structural defects of the consent regime. When the countervailing interests at issue include business interests and the business in question requires pervasive surveillance, the protective power of consent will be undermined. Similarly, where user-generated content is so central to the business model then the distinction between how the users interact both between themselves

---

[20] "Key Facts," *Facebook*, Newsroom, accessed March 5, 2014, available at http://newsroom.fb.com/Key-Facts.

[21] "Advertising," *Facebook*, Newsroom, accessed March 5, 2014, available at http://newsroom.fb.com/Advertising.

[22] "Facebook Reports Third Quarter 2013 Results," *Facebook*, Investor Relations, accessed March 5, 2014, available at http://investor.fb.com/releasedetail.cfm?ReleaseID=802760.

and with the business becomes blurred in important ways not well caught by the consent model.

One of the complaints concerned the lack of an opt-out for targeted advertisements. However, the Assistant Commissioner accepted that it was reasonable that Facebook require consent to advertising as a condition of service. Because Facebook provided its service for free, "advertising is essential to the provision of the service, and persons who wish to use the service must be willing to receive a certain amount of advertising."[23] This is interesting, as one of the applicable interpretive principles of PIPEDA states that individuals should not have to consent to the collection, use, or disclosure of their information "beyond that required to fulfill the explicitly specified and legitimate purposes."[24] This principle could have been understood to impose an obligation on Facebook to provide a version of its services for a fee, should a person wish to opt-out of the targeted ads. By instead understanding the service offered as a "free" service, which in turn requires advertising revenue, which in turn relies upon user data, the principles that are meant to *limit* the collection, use, or disclosure of personal information instead facilitate it by building broad data collection into the "legitimate purpose."

[23] "Report of Findings into the Complaint Filed by the Canadian Internet Policy and Public Interest Clinic (CIPPIC) against Facebook Inc. Under the Personal Information Protection and Electronic Documents Act" (July 16, 2009), para. 131. (Facebook decision)

[24] PIPEDA, Principle 4.3.3.

This signals quite a profound change in how consent-based privacy legislation addresses information practices associated with advertising. In one of the earliest decisions regarding PIPEDA, the Privacy Commissioner of Canada held that Air Canada needed to adopt an explicit opt-in consent mechanism in relation to the targeting marketing associated with its Aeroplan frequent flyer program.[25] Implicit consent was acceptable in relation to the basic workings of the plan, where consumers collect Aeroplan miles and then redeem them for various products and services. But where this departed from the information practices associated with the basic workings of the plan, separate and explicit consent was required. The Facebook decision, in contrast, denies that targeted marketing is a secondary use of information. By accepting Facebook's business model of a free service fueled by advertising revenue, the Assistant Commissioner accepted a business model that requires broad customer surveillance and thus builds this in to the very ideas of legitimate and reasonable purposes. And from there it is a very short step to the key inversion – instead of requiring separate individual consent to surveillance for advertising purposes, individuals are required to consent to advertising *in order to receive services*.

The centrality of user-generated content also played a large role in the decision. Much of the information that Facebook deals with is provided by users in the course of their interactions with each other through Facebook's

---

[25] PIPED Act Case Summary #42 (2002).

platform rather than with Facebook directly as an organization. This makes the social norms of users within their social sphere highly relevant to the privacy questions associated with Facebook. However, these differ from general social norms in two ways. First, these are not general social norms regarding privacy that are formed independently of user experiences and practices on Facebook, but are expectations directly related to Facebook activities and often formed through participation in those activities. Second, both the architectural and business choices that Facebook makes exert a strong influence on the formation of these expectations and Facebook's choices occur within the context of a business model premised on broad information collection and use.

All of these factors affect the consent inquiry in important ways. For example, CIPPIC complained about Facebook's default privacy settings, arguing that they did not conform to previous Canadian decisions regarding consent. The Assistant Commissioner did not see this as determinative, arguing that:

> Unlike individuals in earlier cases, Facebook users proactively and voluntarily upload their personal information to the Facebook site for the express purpose of sharing it with others.[26]

The standard default of information sharing with "My Network and Friend" was reasonable, given that the basic

[26] Facebook decision, para. 88.

infrastructure of Facebook is built around the idea of "friend."[27] Therefore the form of consent (opt-in vs. opt-out) is determined by reference to the reasonable expectations of the users but these expectations themselves are formed by the social media architecture that is meant to facilitate sharing.

These general expectations of users, formed through the active architectural choices of Facebook, can even undercut individual consent entirely. For example, CIPPC complained that Facebook does not provide users with the ability to opt-out of profile memorialization. Although the Assistant Commissioner originally found this to contravene the consent requirements, she changed her view due to "reasonable expectations" with respect to consent:

> In my view, most typical Facebook users would welcome the prospect of being posthumously remembered and honored by their friends on the site. Likewise, I am sure that users generally would regard the freedom to pay their respects to deceased friends and fellow users as an important part of the Facebook experience.[28]

Because of this, the Assistant Commissioner found that Facebook could rely upon implied consent. However, this implied consent is based on what "typical" users would want,

---

[27] Facebook decision, para. 90. The Assistant Commissioner came to a different conclusion regarding the default setting for photo albums, because this was set to "Everyone": paras. 92–95.

[28] Facebook decision, para. 279.

and indeed what "users generally" would want in relation to another individual. There is no opt-out for individuals who wish to make different choices, making it a necessary aspect of the service provided. Reasonable expectations of the "Facebook experience" trump individual consent.

Despite the importance of Facebook's infrastructure in shaping user expectations, Facebook has no obligation to change its infrastructure so as to better enable individual choice. For example, CIPPIC also complained about Facebook users tagging non-users in photographs, which allows their personal information to be disseminated without their knowledge or consent. The only way for non-users to un-tag themselves is to join Facebook; Facebook allows users to provide the email of non-users tagged in photos so that Facebook can send a notification to the non-user inviting them to join Facebook. The Assistant Commissioner held that the responsibility for obtaining non-user consent lies with the person tagging, not with Facebook. However, the collection of email addresses for the purposes of inviting non-users to Facebook also serves Facebook's interests in increasing its membership, so Facebook has some responsibility in relation to the disclosure of email addresses. Facebook had to take "appropriate steps to ensure that users are well aware that they must obtain non-users' consent before disclosing their email addresses to Facebook."[29] What the law does not require, but which would provide more privacy, is that

---

[29] Facebook decision, para. 313.

Facebook provide an infrastructure that is also respective of non-users' rights by allowing non-users to remove tags without joining Facebook.

The corporate-state nexus: lawful access

If consent provides illusory consumer protection in the face of surveillance-as-a-business model, it also does surprising damage in the context of lawful access to that treasure trove of consumer information. I will look at two examples of lawful access. The first concerns a series of cases that considered whether the police required a warrant to obtain subscriber information from internet service providers. The second concerns a series of decisions regarding outsourcing and the question of whether US law provides a comparable level of privacy protection as Canadian law, especially in light of lawful access provisions of US legislation such as the USA Patriot Act. In both examples the structural defects of the consent model play an unexpected and privacy-limiting role.

PIPEDA allows organizations to voluntarily disclose the personal information of its customers without consent for law enforcement purposes.[30] There have been a number of cases where police have requested basic subscriber information from ISPs without a warrant and this warrantless access was challenged as unconstitutional. The cases therefore focus on the actions of the state and are argued in terms of

[30] PIPEDA, s.7.

constitutional law. Nonetheless the combination of PIPEDA's exceptions to consent for law enforcement purposes and ideas of individual consent operate to diminish constitutional protection. I will show this by discussing some of the details of what I take to be the most privacy-protective decision of this type so far – the Ontario Court of Appeal decision in *R v. Ward*.

There are several important privacy-protective aspects to *Ward*. The court accepted that individuals can have a reasonable expectation of privacy in subscriber information, and appreciated the role that this information plays in identifying individuals who would otherwise remain anonymous in their online activities. The court also reiterated Canada's long-standing rejection of the US third-party doctrine from cases such as *Smith v. Maryland* and held that just because an ISP is willing to provide this information to the police does not mean that the police are absolved of their constitutional obligation to obtain a warrant.

These aspects of the decision look like a strong affirmation of the distinctive sphere of constitutional law in governing the individual–state relationship. Where constitutional law begins to bleed into data protection law is in the court's discussion of both PIPEDA and the contractual terms between the ISP and the accused.

The court held that because the legislation "speaks to the circumstances in which the third party holder of the information may disclose that information to the police," this informs the reasonable expectation of privacy analysis and diminishes that expectation. The court might have interpreted the lawful access exemptions to individual consent as speaking only to the individual-organization relationship, shielding the organization from liability when it cooperates with the state. Instead, the court interprets the lawful access exception to change the general social context within which an individual chooses to share information with an organization, undermining an individual's expectations in relation to the state.

The place where the consent-based privacy model does the most damage, however, is in the court's analysis of the terms of the service agreement and how they undermine a reasonable expectation of privacy. According to the court, "the contractual terms speak both of [the ISP's] duty to protect the privacy of clients' information and its willingness to disclose information in relation to investigations involving the alleged criminal misuse of its services."[31] Here we have contractual terms, which are in no realistic sense "negotiated" with a customer, that operate to diminish the rights that the customer has in relation to the state. This analysis uses the organizational relationship and the role of consent to discount constitutional privacy rights.

The second area where the consent-based paradigm has operated to undermine privacy protection in the context of lawful access is in relation to outsourcing. Many Canadian companies – and public institutions – have relationships with US corporations that involve the personal information

---

[31] Facebook decision, para. 107.

of Canadians collected by these organizations crossing the border for processing and/or storage in the United States. In some provincial jurisdictions, regulated organizations must store personal information within Canada unless certain conditions are met.[32] However, most privacy legislation is silent on the question of outsourcing. Although there are differences between these various statutes, the overall shared position is that outsourcing is permissible so long as the privacy protection in another jurisdiction is comparable.

It is in this comparison that, oddly enough, the consent-based view of privacy asserts itself to undermine privacy. If one thinks that privacy is about individual control, then disclosure without consent is the chief privacy violation to be concerned about. To compare jurisdictions, one would look at whether there are similar provisions for disclosure to state authorities without consent. Consider the following statement of the Information and Privacy Commissioner of Ontario, which is representative of these outsourcing decisions:

> I understand the complainant's concern that the PATRIOT Act may be used by U.S. Law enforcement agencies to access Ontarians' personal information. However, the risk that law enforcement agencies may access personal information is not restricted to information held in the U.S. In fact, Canadian law enforcement agencies have similarly robust legal powers to obtain personal information held in Canada,

---

[32] Freedom of Information and Protection of Privacy Act RSBC 1996 ch. 165, s.30.1.

and similar powers exist throughout most counties in the world. Further, law enforcement agencies in Canada, the U.S. and other countries have the ability to reach across borders to access personal information under various laws and agreements.[33]

The focus here is entirely on whether state authorities have powers to obtain personal information.

There is a striking omission in this analysis, however. A constitutional lawyer looking at the question of "similar powers" to compel access would not focus on *whether* such powers existed or not. The constitutional question regarding compelled state access is: access on what standards? When we ask that question then important differences emerge between the United States and Canada.

One set of differences concern the standard that applies for authorization of a warrant. Canada, like the United States, usually requires "reasonable and probable grounds to believe that an offence has been committed and that evidence of the offence is to be found at the place of the search."[34] It is also true that in Canada, like the United States, national security laws dilute this standard. However, there are important differences. To take just one example, section 215 of the USA Patriot Act requires "reasonable grounds to believe that the tangible things sought are relevant to an authorized

---

[33] PC12–39, p.5. For similar views expressed in relation to PIPEDA, see: #2005–313, #2007–365, #2008–394.

[34] *Hunter v. Southam*, 2 SCR 144 (1984), 168.

investigation."[35] In contrast, section 21 of the CSIS Act requires reasonable grounds to believe that a warrant is required to enable an investigation authorized under the Act and "that other investigative procedures have been tried and have failed," or that there is some special urgency. The Canadian act is therefore more privacy protective.

The outsourcing decisions also fail to make the right comparison. The important comparison is between Canadians under Canadian law and Canadians under US law, *not* Canadians under Canadian law and Americans under US law. Once we make this comparison, it becomes clear that there are many prohibitions on targeting Canadians under Canadian law that do not have an analogue in US law – indeed, provisions like section 702 of FISA provide for rather broad powers of surveillance in relation to non-US persons and do not have a Canadian counterpart. Moreover, many of the provisions in US law that are meant to protect privacy and freedom of expression apply only to US persons. Another set of differences concern what kind of information attracts a "reasonable expectation of privacy" under constitutional law. As already discussed, Canadian courts have long rejected the US third-party doctrine. Finally, although there are indeed Mutual Assistance Treaties that permit cooperation across borders, they ensure that it is domestic search and seizure standards that apply, not the standards of another country.

---

[35] Codified as 50 USC 1861(b)(2)(A).

The consent paradigm leaves decision-makers who operate primarily within the data-protection law world without the conceptual resources to ask the right questions. Without seeing the constitutional dimensions to lawful access, these outsourcing decisions have actually facilitated state surveillance on less protective – and even unconstitutional – standards.

An alternative paradigm: power

The previous examples illustrate the need to think carefully about the intersection of different spheres of privacy, and their attendant privacy models, with fair information practices and their emphasis on individual control and consent. The problem is this: consent cannot bear the load it is supposed to, but other ideas of privacy are both drawn from different social spheres with different characteristic relationships and seem deficient in the face of contemporary information practices because of their emphasis on ideas of intimacy, secrecy, confidentiality, or private places. We need a new source of privacy inspiration.

I want to propose a very different way of thinking about privacy, but one that retains some deep affinities with the individual-consent model. The consent model is frequently described either in terms of property or in terms of strengthening it through making it more like property.[36] I disagree

---

[36] See, e.g., Policy Department, Citizens' Rights and Constitutional Affairs, "National programs for mass surveillance of personal data in EU Member States and their compatibility with EU law" (2013) at

with turning privacy rights into property rights. Nonetheless, I argue that there are two significant, and overlooked, lessons that privacy law can take from property, and in particular from our ideas of trespass. First, the trespass roots of constitutional guarantees against unreasonable search and seizure point us to the importance of basic rule-of-law values that have long underpinned the constitutional right to privacy. We need much more explicit attention to these values, along with an understanding of the role that private sector organizations, and citizens more generally, play in both upholding them and being constrained by them. I call this the "power-over" analysis. Second, private-law trespass rules are instructive for they show us that trespass is not about harm but about legal powers. An understanding of legal powers can point us to the important role that law plays in facilitating our ability to do things that we otherwise would not be able to do rather than protecting us from harms. I call this the "power-to" analysis. Together, they offer a set of resources for thinking about the obligations that information intermediaries might have in relation to their customers beyond simply securing consent.

One of the benefits of focusing on both power-over and power-to is that it shifts the focus of privacy protection away from the individual and places it on the surveilling party. For example, if we start from the position that it is up to individuals to determine their own privacy preferences, then the

p. 7; James Rule, "Toward Strong Privacy: Values, Markets, Mechanisms, and Institutions," *University of Toronto Law Journal* 54 (2004), 183.

obligation of someone seeking to collect information from that individual is to obtain consent. If instead we start from the position that surveillance places the surveilling party in a position of power over another then the obligations of the surveilling party might be quite different. The law in most contemporary liberal democracies regulates power relationships across a wide variety of contexts in a wide variety of ways. Labor law offers a rich set of examples, with both collective bargaining regimes and employment standards offering ways of intervening in asymmetric power relationships involved in many labor markets. Choice and consent are not the central ideas in such examples; instead they involve a recognition of the limits of the ideas of individual choice and consent when these are operationalized without sensitivity to the power dynamics that can substantively undermine individual interests even as they are formally protected.[37] We need not be confined to ideas of power-over in order to understand how surveilling parties might incur obligations. Sometimes to be empowered to do something relies upon the availability of social and institutional structures that provide the conditions for this, which can in turn impose positive obligations on others to play a role in supporting those structures.[38] This is part of

---

[37] One can recognize the limits of individual choice and still argue for the value of individual autonomy overall. Employment standards can support autonomy even as they force terms in employment contracts.

[38] Robert Post makes an argument like this when he writes that privacy is about protecting social norms of civility. See Post, "The Social Foundations of Privacy."

what I am calling power-to. Taken together, I argue, this focus on power offers fruitful resources for thinking through the challenges facing privacy law.

Constraining power: rule-of-law lessons from constitutional law

Search and seizure laws used to be rooted in ideas of trespass and I want to suggest that there is something very important here that has been lost sight of in the move from ideas of property to ideas of privacy as the animating analytical idea. That something is the rule of law.

One of the great historical search and seizure cases from the United Kingdom, *Entick v. Carrington*, shows how ideas of trespass and the rule of law are intertwined.[39] Entick had been accused of seditious libel, and the general warrant issued was sweeping in its breadth. He brought a trespass action in relation to the search of his house and, in finding for Entick, the court made its very famous proclamation regarding private property:

> [O]ur law holds the property of every man so sacred, that no man can set his foot upon his neighbour's close without his leave; if he does he is a trespasser, though he does no damage at all; if he will tread upon his neighbour's ground, he must justify it by law.

One can also read this statement from the perspective of a concern for the arbitrary exercise of state authority. State

---

[39] *Entick v. Carrington* (1765), 95 ER 807 (KB).

authorities must act within the law – including the law of trespass – unless they have special justification.

The court did not think the general warrant in this case had such justification, very much because of concerns regarding the unfettered discretion arising from a lack of procedural fairness and accountability. According to the court:

> The warrant in our case was an execution in the first instance, without any previous summons, examination, hearing the plaintiff, or proof that he was the author of the supposed libels; a power claimed by no other magistrate whatever . . .; it was left to the discretion of these defendants to execute the warrant in the absence or presence of the plaintiff, when he might have no witness present to see what they did; for they were to seize all papers, bank bills or any other valuable papers they might take away if they were so disposed; there might be nobody to detect them.

This concern regarding discretionary authority was one of the key concerns animating search and seizure law, influencing the adoption of the US Fourth Amendment, as well as the law in other jurisdictions.[40] Unfortunately, we have largely lost that explicit focus through the shift to the language of a reasonable expectation of privacy.

[40] Thomas Y. Davies, "Recovering the Original Fourth Amendment," *Michigan Law Review* 98 (1999), 547; The Honorable M. Blane Michael, "Reading the Fourth Amendment: Guidance From the Mischief that Gave it Birth," *NYU Law Review* 85 (2010), 905; Lisa M. Austin, "Getting Past Privacy? Surveillance, the *Charter*, and the Rule of Law," *Canadian Journal of Law and Society* 27 (2013), 381.

Privacy law in the constitutional realm would therefore benefit from looking to rule-of-law values. One way to do this is to retreat back to an explicit property focus.[41] My approach is different, however. The lesson from the trespass roots of search and seizure is a lesson about the rule of law generally and not property specifically. A broad rule-of-law approach would focus on the surveilling party and questions of power, its possibility of abuse, and legal safeguards. It would place questions of transparency and accountability at the center of the debate rather than as add-ons to the reasonable expectation of privacy analysis.

The issue is one of reclamation rather than reinvention. A very recent example of the power of this approach is the *Obama v. Klayman* decision.[42] Justice Leon stated, after acknowledging that other courts have come to other conclusions regarding the privacy of metadata:

> [A]s the Supreme Court notes more than a decade before *Smith*, "[t]he basic purpose of th[e Fourth] Amendment, as recognized in countless decisions of this Court, is to safeguard the privacy and security of individuals against *arbitrary invasions by governmental officials*." *Camara v. Mun. Court*, 387 U.S. 523, 528 (1967) ... The Fourth Amendment

---

[41] *United States v. Jones*, 132 S. Ct. 945(2012); Morgan Cloud, "The Fourth Amendment During the Lochner Era: Privacy, Property, and Liberty in Constitutional Theory," *Stanford Law Review* 48 (1996), 555.

[42] *Klayman v. Obama* (2013) No. 13–0851 U.S. District Court, District of Columbia.

typically requires "a neutral and detached authority be interposed between the police and the public," and it is offended by "general warrants" and laws that allow searches to be conducted "indiscriminately and without regard to their connection with [a] crime under investigation." *Berger v. New York*, 388 U.S. 41, 54, 59 (1967). I cannot imagine a more "indiscriminate" and "arbitrary invasion" than this systematic and high-tech collection and retention of personal data on virtually every single citizen for purposes of querying and analyzing it without prior judicial approval.[43]

It is the arbitrariness of the methods that offended Justice Leon and it is not surprising that, in order to articulate this, he revived explicit rule-of-law language.

It is not just broad state surveillance, unmoored from particularized suspicion, which is problematic from a rule-of-law perspective. The combination of broad surveillance and broad law enforcement discretion also is concerning. As many civil liberties groups have long argued, given the large number of laws on the books and the wide discretion given to prosecutors, the more surveillance we have, the more likely people will be subject to the threat of prosecution. This threat can operate in various ways: it can lead to problematic discrimination and manipulation on the part of law enforcement agents, and it can have an inhibiting effect on citizens more generally.[44] We might be able to articulate this through the

[43] *Klayman*, 63–64 (original emphasis).
[44] See Neil Richards, "The Dangers of Surveillance," *Harvard Law Review* 126 (2013).

language of a reasonable expectation of privacy, but a rule-of-law focus makes the point about abuse of discretion more directly. Moreover, it shifts the focus away from individual harms to the broader systemic concerns of what it means to demand to live in a society where the law rules.

More importantly for the purposes of this chapter, a rule-of-law focus can provide a new way of thinking about the obligations of citizens and organizations and their relationship to state authorities. Although it is quite standard to think of questions of accountability in quite hierarchical terms, where the courts hold agents of the state to account, other private actors within the state also play an important role.

Postema has made this point recently, arguing that we cannot think of accountability in terms of a chain that terminates in an unaccountable accountability-holder like Hobbes' sovereign.[45] We can have unaccountable wielders of power, he argues, but accountability-holders must themselves be held accountable. This is possible if we think of accountability in terms of a network, where it is shared and distributed throughout the community by all its various members. Members of the community have a corresponding responsibility to exercise this power, a responsibility that is both mutual and general, and that "each member owes to each

---

[45] Gerald Postema, "Fidelity in Law's Commonwealth," in *Private Law and the Rule of Law*, eds. Lisa M. Austin & Dennis Klimchuk (Oxford University Press, 2014), forthcoming.

other member and to all."[46] Citizens therefore play a role in holding each other and the state accountable, and we should not construe this only in terms of democratic accountability. Citizens are vital to the maintenance of a state subject to the rule of law.

There are multiple dimensions to this role, but I want to flag three here. The first issue is the role of trust. Law enforcement has historically relied upon citizen cooperation in its investigations and trust plays a large role in this cooperation. When a community trusts its authorities, it is more willing to cooperate with them; when trust fails, cooperation declines. Consider the following example. When Canadian authorities recently thwarted an alleged terrorist plot to bomb a Via Rail train it was with help from the Canadian Muslim community.[47] This help, in turn, was facilitated by a concerted effort on the part of the RCMP to improve its relationship with the Muslim community by making friends and building trust.[48] Therefore, the willingness to come forward is tied to a sense of trust and that sense of trust must be earned within a community through the active building of relationships. Trust turns out to be an important

---

[46] Emphasis removed.

[47] Colin Freeze, "How faith built a fragile trust between police, Muslim community," *Globe and Mail* (April 25, 2013), accessed March 5, 2014, available at http://www.theglobeandmail.com/news/national/how-faith-built-a-fragile-trust-between-police-muslim-community/article11540816.

[48] Freeze, "How faith built a fragile trust".

accountability mechanism – authorities need to maintain trust in order to maintain cooperation, so that we can have effective law enforcement.

We can think of this trust in general terms but it also arises in specific contexts. A request for information from individuals within a community long characterized by poor relationships with authorities is one that will suffer for lack of general trust. However, a request for information might meet with a more specific distrust if the individual has grounds to suspect that the request is arbitrary or unfair in some specific manner. For example, requests to internet service providers for subscriber information that look like broad fishing expeditions, perhaps because of their frequency or lack of reasons, rather than tied to specific investigations with articulable grounds of suspicion, might raise this kind of specific distrust. This is directly related to the rule-of-law concern regarding constraining the exercise of arbitrary authority. Even if the request is one that the police do not need a warrant to make, a suspicion of arbitrariness is a legitimate basis for refusal.

The second issue regarding the relationship between citizens and the rule of law is the role that citizens play in exercising judgment with respect to the accountability of others. We do not just decide when to cooperate with state authorities once they approach us for that cooperation. We also decide when to *seek* state intervention, sometimes in relation to the vindication of our own rights and sometimes in relation to reporting the infractions of others. In this we all exercise judgment, and sometimes mercy and forgiveness. We decide when things are serious and in need of state intervention, when they can be worked out in other ways, and when they represent lapses in judgment to be overlooked or forgiven.

I think this provides another way of thinking about the areas of "permitted deviance" that Alan Westin discusses in his intriguing remarks regarding the emotional release secured by privacy. One element of this release, he claims, is the freedom of noncompliance with social norms:

> Some norms are formally adopted–perhaps as law–which society really expects many persons to break. This ambivalence produces a situation in which almost everyone does break some social or institutional norms–for example, violating traffic laws, breaking sexual mores, cheating on expense accounts, overstating income-tax deductions, or smoking in rest rooms when this is prohibited. Although society will usually punish the most flagrant abuses, it tolerates the great bulk of the violations as "permissible" deviations. If there were no privacy to permit society to ignore these deviations–if all transgressions were known–most persons in society would be under organizational discipline or in jail, or could be manipulated by threats of such action. The firm expectation of having privacy for permissible deviations is a distinguishing characteristic of life in a free society.[49]

It is true that some of our traditional spheres of privacy – such as privacy of the home – allow us a place of social experimentation, or permissible deviation, free from observation. But

[49] Alan Westin, *Privacy and Freedom* (New York: Atheneum, 1967), 35.

another aspect of this is those deviations for which there are observers. There are a broad and complex set of norms and practices, social relationships, individual decisions, and values that keep individuals from reporting these infractions.

Allow me to connect this broadly to the rule of law and then make a few observations regarding information intermediaries. A traditional rule-of-law concern is the followability of laws. Fuller argues that laws should not demand the impossible, while others have argued for a broader view of this.[50] Similarly, Simonds argues that the law should be compatible with a viable way of life,[51] and Oakeshott argues that the law should not conflict with a certain "prevailing educated moral sensibility."[52] There is a rule-of-law problem, therefore, when laws are not followable by a community. This might be especially true when social norms are in transition and begin to depart from formal laws. Citizens could then play a role in resisting the enforcement of these formal laws, and could do so in multiple ways.[53] But it is also true in much more mundane circumstances where various other social

---

[50] Lon L. Fuller, *The Morality of Law* (New Haven: Yale University Press, 1969), 70ff.

[51] Nigel Simmonds, *Law as a Moral Idea* (Oxford: Oxford University Press, 2007).

[52] Michael Oakeshott, "The Rule of Law" in *On History and Other Essays* (Oxford: Basil Blackwell, 1983), 160.

[53] A dramatic example of this is how Canadian juries refused to convict Dr. Henry Morgentaler despite the fact that the evidence clearly showed that he was performing what were then illegal abortions in his clinics in the 1970s.

norms and context-specific knowledge mean that individuals turn a blind eye to certain kinds of deviations. If everything we do is perfectly transparent to the state, then this mediating role played by other citizens is undercut.

If we accept that citizens have a role to play in upholding the rule of law then we should also be worried about the shift in policing methods to make increasing use of the vast repositories of information currently collected by information intermediaries. This shift diminishes both traditional practical constraints on arbitrary behavior as well as the active role that citizens play in deciding when to cooperate with, and even when to initiate, state intervention.[54] Where investigatory methods are resource intensive, and where they have a direct impact on community relations because of their visibility, arbitrary targeting is less likely to occur. Increased reliance on new surveillance technologies destroys these practical constraints.[55] The other constraint that is undermined in this shift is the role played by citizen

[54] For a discussion of shifting methods, see Kevin D. Haggerty, Dean Wilson, & Gavin J.D. Smith, "Theorizing surveillance in crime control," *Theoretical Criminology* 15 (2011), 213–217.

[55] This is similar to the "practical obscurity" arguments sometimes made in privacy debates, where it is recognized that old technologies like paper records stored in physical files in multiple locations offer individuals more privacy than when these same records are electronic and stored in databases that may be centralized or linked through networks. The shift in technology destroys the "practical obscurity" maintained by the paper files and calls for new thinking about privacy. The argument here has a similar structure except that it is about "practical constraints."

engagement. For example, if video cameras pointed at public places are ubiquitous and law enforcement has easy access to their footage,[56] then there is no need for the police to ask for the voluntary cooperation of citizens on the street. But the removal of this role also means the removal of the various roles that citizens play in ensuring the accountability of both the state and fellow citizens.

Even information intermediaries are removed from much of this, or at least a multinational internet company doing business over the web is significantly different in terms of its contextual civic understanding than a small business operating in a local neighborhood. It is striking that in Canada, to the extent that it has been measured, only 6.4 percent of requests for basic customer information from the RCMP (in non-child exploitation cases) were refused in the absence of a warrant.[57]

---

[56] This is like the scenario feared in relation to city surveillance centers in the United States. See Darwin BondGraham & Ali Winston, "The Real Purpose of Oakland's Surveillance Center," *East Vat Express*, accessed March 5, 2014, available at http://m.eastbayexpress.com/oakland/the-real-purpose-of-oaklands-surveillance-center/Content?issue=3789180&oid=3789230. However, there are important legal questions here, which I am ignoring. The police use of CCTV cameras is regulated in Canada by public sector privacy legislation as well as the constitution. Access to the footage from private cameras is regulated in the same way that access to subscriber information is – the obligations of the private organization are regulated through PIPEDA, and the obligations of the police in requiring a warrant or not are regulated through the constitution.

[57] Sgt. Bernard Tremblay, "Basic Subscriber Information (CAN) 2010" October 25, 2011 (on file with author).

The routine cooperation with state authorities, in the context of policing that is removed from a community context, diminishes the role of citizens in holding each other, and the state, to account. All of this suggests the need for new thinking regarding accountability, where different configurations of transparency and participation can replace our old structures.

The third issue regarding the relationship between citizens and the rule of law, which I will discuss in more detail below in relation to the revision of fair information practices, is that the rule of law is not confined to constraining public power if by this we mean exercises of state authority against individuals. A growing amount of scholarship also emphasizes the role played by the rule of law in many spheres of private law, involving the relationship between individuals.[58] As Robin West has argued, this may even be one of the most important aspects of the rule of law.[59] The focus of power-over, therefore, and the rule-of-law framework that it suggests, can inform how we think about the relationship between individuals and information intermediaries as well as about the relationship between individuals and the state as mediated by these organizations.

---

[58] Lisa M. Austin, "Property and the Rule of Law," *Legal Theory*, forthcoming; See also essays in Lisa M. Austin & Dennis Klimchuk, eds., *Private Law and the Rule of Law*.

[59] Robin West, "The Limits of Process" in James E. Fleming (ed.), *Getting to the Rule of Law: NOMOS L.* (New York University Press, 2011), 45.

Enabling power: lessons from private property

Individual control over a sphere of information has many similarities to property norms and it is no surprise that there are sometimes calls for property rights for personal information.[60] I think that property law has a number of lessons to offer to privacy theory but these lessons do not lie in reviving some idea of a bounded sphere over which an individual has control and in relation to which an individual requires protection from invasions. Rather, these lessons lie in the relation between private property and power.

Much has been written about one aspect of this relationship, namely the power relations between those who have property and those who do not. Because private property allows individuals to act in their own self-interest in relation to their property, asymmetrical concentrations of property facilitate relationships of domination. These debates are important, but I would characterize them in terms of the power-over discussion of the previous section. In other words, I think that the important element to emphasize is the rule-of-law story regarding constraints on power.[61] My focus in this section is on a different aspect of power associated with property – the idea of a legal power, or what I call "power-to." I argue that the lesson we should take from

---

[60] Paul M. Schwartz, "Property, Privacy, and Personal Data," *Harvard Law Review* 117 (2004), 2055; James Rule, "Toward Strong Privacy: Values, Markets, Mechanisms, and Institutions," *University of Toronto Law Journal* 42 (2004), 183.

[61] Postema, "Fidelity in Law's Commonwealth."

trespass is that property is primarily concerned with legal powers rather than legal wrongs and that this is an instructive lesson to take up in relation to privacy debates.

Trespass is a tort concerned with a particular kind of wrongdoing – the interference with the right of possession. However, trespass is not an injury-based tort; there is no need to prove damages in order to prevail.[62] An injunction is the preferred remedy, but where damages are argued the measure of damages is not a loss that must be made good but the amount that the rightful possessor would have charged for the use at issue had this been bargained for. Both the preference for an injunction restraining the interference and the measure of damages reflecting the value of the use, rather than a loss to the possessor, reflect the nature of the right of possession as one of exclusive control. An injunction prevents others from using my property without my permission; as a second-best option, damages make the trespasser pay me for their use. In contrast, an injury-based rule would allow others to use my property without my permission and without payment so long as they did not cause me injury. This would seriously undermine the very idea of exclusive possession.

Sometimes arguments are made to the effect that if another uses my property without my permission and does not pay for it then this does cause me injury – an injury to my ability to charge for that use. But this mixes up two things

---

[62] Trespass to chattels is an exception. See *Intel v. Hamidi*, 30 Cal. 4th 1342 (2003).

that are important to keep distinct: actions that make me worse off in light of my present state of affairs and interests, and actions that prevent me from exercising some right in the future that might make me better off. Damaging my house falls within the former, walking across my property without asking my permission falls within the latter.

Much of property is concerned with these future-oriented abilities. Property rights allow us to do things that we otherwise could not. They are, in H. L. A. Hart's classic sense, legal powers.[63] As he argued, these are distinct from legal rules that impose obligations. Instead, legal rules that define how to make a valid will confer powers that "provide individuals with facilities for realizing their wishes."[64] We can imagine a legal regime without powers of alienation, for example, but individuals living in such a jurisdiction are not *harmed* because they lack such powers even if we think they would be better off by having them. Harms and injuries are about setbacks to our current actual interests. Measured against the current state of affairs, a harm is something that makes us worse off. In contrast, powers provide us with abilities we otherwise do not have. Measured against the current state of affairs, having a power makes us better off but not having it does not make us worse off.

---

[63] For a more extended defence of this idea, see Lisa M. Austin, "The Power of the Rule of Law," in *Private Law and the Rule of Law*, eds. Lisa M. Austin & Dennis Klimchuk.

[64] H. L. A. Hart, *The Concept of Law* (Oxford: Clarendon Press, 1961), 27–29.

The framework of tort liability often leads us to think in terms of wrongs, and the injuries that flow from these wrongs, rather than in terms of powers and the way in which these facilitate actions we could not otherwise accomplish. This framework has exerted a strong influence on our thinking about privacy law ever since Warren and Brandeis' famous essay. What I propose here is that we think of privacy in terms of powers rather than in terms of wrongs, and liberate privacy thinking from its search for privacy harms. This focus on harm has been deeply problematic for privacy. As Solove has noted, "[m]ost privacy problems lack dead bodies," and this lack leads people to think that privacy is at stake only "when something deeply embarrassing or discrediting is revealed."[65]

One of the benefits of rejecting a wrongs-based approach to privacy is that it takes us away from the view that privacy rights protect us against "invasions." This is the kind of view that leads to an emphasis on spheres of privacy, such as the home, or spheres of informational secrecy, such as confidential and sensitive information. A "power-to" focus can show that privacy norms do not secure our conditions of social withdrawal within a private sphere so much as they secure our conditions of social interaction.[66]

---

[65] Daniel Solove, "'I've Got Nothing to Hide' and Other Misunderstandings of Privacy," *San Diego Law Review* 44 (2007), 745, 768–769.

[66] Julie E. Cohen, *Configuring the Networked Self: Law, Code, and the Play of Everyday Practice* (New Haven, Conn.: Yale University Press, 2012); Valerie Steeves, "Reclaiming the Social Value of

There are, no doubt, different ways to think about privacy in such terms. Let me offer one such account here, as an illustration. Privacy norms secure our ability – let's call it our power – of self-presentation. As Goffman argued, individuals "present" themselves in social interactions.[67] For Goffman, the individual self simply is the "performed character" that emerges from this presentation, dependent for its emergence on a number of social structures and the roles played by other people.[68] Although I do not want to take such a strong view regarding the nature of the self, Goffman's views are helpful for understanding our social identity and the role played by other people in what is a dynamic social process.

Three aspects to the role played by other people in relation to an individual's self-presentation are worth noting. The first is the importance of audience segregation. For Goffman, individuals present themselves *to others*, and who those others are is important. Through self-presentation an individual seeks to define a situation in order to try to control others' "responsive treatment of him."[69] Audience segregation is important, which includes segregation from "outsiders" or people who are not part of the intended, and

Privacy," *in Lessons From the Identity Trail: Anonymity, Privacy and Identity in a Networked Society*, Ian Kerr, Valerie Steeves, & Carole Lucock, eds. (Oxford University Press, 2009).

[67] Erving Goffman, *The Presentation of Self in Everyday Life* (New York: Doubleday Anchor, 1959).

[68] *Ibid.*, 253.

[69] *Ibid.*, 3.

expected, audience, as well as segregation between the audience and the "back-stage," where preparations for the performance are made.[70] Rebecca Tushnet provides a wonderful illustration of the ways in which pseudonyms are a method of managing one's audience, and therefore one's self-presentation. As she points out, this enables connection, not isolation.

The second important feature of the role other people play is that the audience is not passive but participates actively in a performance. The audience itself seeks to maintain the definition of the performance.[71] The audience does this through various forms of "tact" which include ways in which audiences themselves seek to uphold audience segregation.[72]

Third, audience expectations highlight the importance of well-understood props and social roles available to a performer. As Goffman is at pains to stress, social interaction involves performers seeking to define a situation within an inter-subjective interactional order. An individual performer must rely upon already existing props and social roles in order to define a situation that the audience will understand and accept.[73]

The actions of other people are important in securing our ability of self-presentation. However, if we think that the analogy with legal powers is appropriate, then we do not

[70] *Ibid.*, 135.
[71] Goffman, The Presentation of Self, 9.
[72] *Ibid.*, 49.
[73] *Ibid.*, 75.

have to argue that undermining this ability leads directly to some individual harm. Instead, we can focus on what is necessary to ensure that individuals have this ability, and why they are better off with it than without.

If this is what a power-to account of privacy looks like, how can it reorient our thinking about some of the issues previously discussed? One of the things it does is provide a way of thinking about the obligations other people have in relation to privacy, apart from either securing individual consent to a proposed information practice, or balancing the need for consent against their own interests. For example, it highlights the importance of social norms and social roles. If we understand that information intermediaries play an important role in actually *constituting* these social norms and social roles – through both their business models and architecture – then we can see how this might impart privacy obligations. Similarly, the importance of audience segregation to meaningful self-presentation, and the role information intermediaries play in creating the possibilities of this segregation, suggests that we should think about positive obligations to provide these possibilities. We impose positive obligations across a range of other behavior – building code requirements that ensure health and safety standards or basic accessibility is one example, human rights codes that impose obligations of accommodation are another example. This is not to suggest that it would be easy to get social support for imposing affirmative obligations in this way, only that we have done so in other contexts to which we could draw analogies.

If we understand the active role that the audience plays, and the role of tact, then we can also see that there are reasons why an organization might not want to share information with others despite the fact that it has been shared with them. Tact allows us to ignore even what is in plain view, including what might have been intentionally placed there, in order to maintain the more generally accepted social norms of interaction.[74]

The role of the audience in this inter-subjective interactional order can also provide new insights into a number of issues associated with forms of consumer profiling. In deciding how to present myself to another, I take into account what I think that other person knows about me. In most cases this is a combination of information that I have shared with them and my general reputation. What profiling does is *create* information about me. This might be something that I already know but that I have not chosen to share with you, but which you now infer through analytic techniques. An example of this is Target's pregnancy profile, where they mined customer data in order to determine the shopping habits of women who were pregnant.[75] Sometimes these techniques can be used to infer things about you that you

---

[74] See also Thomas Nagel, "Concealment and Exposure," *Philosophy & Public Affairs* 27 (1998), 3.

[75] Charles Duhigg, "How Companies Learn Your Secrets," *The New York Times* (February 16, 2012), accessed March 5, 2014, available at http://www.nytimes.com/2012/02/19/magazine/shopping-habits.html?pagewanted=all&_r=0.

might not know yourself. As one article describes President Obama's use of big data for his re-election campaign: "The campaign didn't just know who you were; it knew exactly how it could turn you into the type of person it wanted you to be." If you do not know what various organizations know about you, then you are unable to understand the basis upon which they interact with you, which raises the concern of manipulation. Posner prominently argued that privacy allows individuals to act manipulatively by hiding information important to particular social interactions.[76] His argument is overstated, but he nonetheless makes an important point. However, this manipulation works the other way as well, when the person or organization I interact with has access to information about me that I either do not know they have or may not even know exists. As Neil Richards argues, we have to attend to the "power effects" of information use.

This too calls for a kind of transparency, which needs to go beyond the access to personal information that has traditionally been a part of FIPs. What we need is an access regime that allows access of some sort to data profiling techniques.[77] Moreover, we need broad access rights rather than access rights of particular individuals to their own personal information. These profiling techniques affect the broader

---

[76] Richard A. Posner, "The Right of Privacy," *Georgia Law Review* 12 (1978), 393.

[77] Frank Pasquale, "Beyond Innovation and Competition: The Need for Qualified Transparency in Internet Intermediaries," *Northwestern University Law Review* 104 (2010), 105.

social context, the construction of social norms, and the terms upon which various groups interact.

Rethinking the basis of fair information practices

Once we see the importance of an analysis of both power-over and power-to, then we have a new basis with which to examine and rethink the foundations of fair information practices.

The power-to analysis can help in ensuring that fair information practices can address the role that information intermediaries play in constituting the world within which we interact and communicate. Instead of seeing this realm of interpersonal interaction as something separate from what FIPs regulate, we can see the importance of ensuring that our legal rules secure the conditions for self-presentation. We need to broaden our focus beyond consent and understand the importance of audience segregation, audience obligations, and practices of tact, and the role of social norms and roles. We need to understand that, in building our world of social interaction, intermediaries are actively engaged in these processes and this should factor into our understanding of their obligations. The power-to analysis can also provide new ways of thinking about the relationship between the organization and individuals apart from this mediating role. For example, issues related to profiling require creative ways of thinking about the obligations of organizations and the practices of transparency and accountability. There are many others.

The power-over analysis, drawing upon ideas of the rule of law, can help address the role that intermediaries play in regulating access to law enforcement and many aspects of this have already been flagged. However, this analysis is also helpful for understanding the norms that should govern the individual–organization relationship. The rule of law is an ideal that applies within private relationships, even if the way in which this applies is contested.[78] In the remainder of this section I want to make a series of analogies to ideas of the rule of law that are reflected in both public sector information laws and also in how public administrative agencies are regulated. If we accept that some of these ideas can migrate to the private sector, they are a useful source of possibilities and ideas for rethinking of FIPS as they apply to information intermediaries.

One aspect of public sector privacy legislation that is often overlooked in privacy discussions is that many jurisdictions twin this with freedom-of-information legislation.[79] Together, these two types of legislative regimes regulate governmental information practices. One function of freedom of information is to make governments accountable to citizens. This fits within Postema's account, as outlined previously, of the non-hierarchical structure of accountability. Citizens have an important role in holding public power

---

[78] See, for example, the essays on this topic in Lisa M. Austin & Dennis Klimchuk, eds., *Private Law and the Rule of Law.*

[79] In Canada most provinces put privacy and access to information together in provincial legislation.

accountable, and freedom of information enables this.[80] If we accept the importance of access to information in relation to public agencies then we should seriously think about a version of this applying to private sector organizations. As already outlined, there are a variety of arguments one can make for the need for a broader vision of transparency and accountability that goes beyond simply providing individuals with a right of access to their own personal information held by an organization.[81]

What is less obvious is that there are rule-of-law ideas *already* present in public sector privacy legislation. If we take a step back, however, and look at the debate regarding the rule of law and the growth of the administrative state, some of this comes into view. Many state practices regarding information collection, use, and disclosure are in the service of the administrative state. There is a long history of thinking about the relationship between the administrative state and the rule of law generally, albeit within the legal literature and not in relation to information practices. In the surveillance studies literature there is a lot of discussion of the information practices associated with the administrative state.[82] However, there is relatively little attention paid to

[80] Postema, "Fidelity in Law's Commonwealth."
[81] See Frank Pasquale, "Beyond Innovation and Competition."
[82] A classic study is John Gilliom's *Overseers of the Poor: Surveillance, Resistance, and the Limits of Privacy* (Chicago, IL: University of Chicago Press, 2001).

whether administrative law doctrines that have sought to reconcile the administrative state with the rule of law have anything to contribute to debates regarding information practices.[83] These doctrines stress ideas such as procedural fairness and constraints on discretion, taking into account the unique context of administrative decision-making.

Many of the principles of FIPs can be interpreted to ensure that the collection, use, and disclosure of personal information are authorized and remain within the bounds of that authority. Authorization can take many forms, including by the law or by the individual through consent. This ensures that information practices remain bounded by the law.

One key element of administrative law is procedural rights of participation. The basic idea is that the individual should get to participate in important decisions being made about him or her and to have all relevant information considered. We can see a version of this in FIPs and the Individual Participation Principle, which involves the right to know whether a "data controller" has information about an individual, to gain access to that data, to have it corrected if inaccurate, and if denied access then to be able to challenge that denial. The Openness Principle also recognizes a number of aspects of transparency and procedural fairness, stating that "[t]here should be a general policy of openness about

---

[83] Excellent exceptions to this are Danielle Keats Citron's "Technological Due Process," *Washington University Law Review* 85 (2008), 1249 and Julie Cohen's "What Is Privacy For," *Harvard Law Review* 126 (2013).

developments, practices and policies with respect to personal data."[84]

If we recognize that some aspects of FIPs articulate ideas of accountability and procedural fairness, then we open new avenues for thinking about privacy law reform, both in the public and private sectors. For example, FIPs offer a very individualized model, where accountability relates to individual data subjects and their personal information. However, suppose that the government analyzes de-identified data in order to determine a particular kind of risk profile and then uses this risk profile to determine whom to single out for heightened scrutiny. This use of information has an individualized impact, but also a general one, and might rely upon information practices that do not make use of identifiable, and hence "personal," information. There are still important issues of accountability, accuracy, and transparency, although they will require different articulations than our current fair information practices.

Other avenues for thinking about fair information practices in terms of this analogy with administrative law include a focus on the norms of decisional transparency with which administrative bodies exercise rule-making functions. If information practices – including those of information intermediaries – have significant regulatory functions, then perhaps procedural participation rights need to be extended in some manner. Other ideas for exploration include norms of

[84] OECD Guidelines.

reasoned decision-making and reviews of decisions. These are all analogies, but at least highlight a very different set of questions that come into focus once we leave aside a focus on privacy and individual choice and see that there are other important values at stake in these debates.

This analogy with administrative law might be fruitful but we should also not lose sight of the shift of paradigm that is taking place. Information practices are no longer operating within the paradigm of the bureaucratic rationality of the administrative state. As many have pointed out, we are see-ing a shift towards models of prediction and prevention.[85] This is governance through profiling and categorization, where governments and organizations seek to predict what you are likely to do and try to regulate this future action. Our traditional ideas regarding the relationship between law and guidance are at odds with this picture. For example, if I know that it is illegal to bring a weapon on board a plane then I can avoid legal liability by avoiding this act. But if I want to avoid being on a no-fly list then I need to know the basis upon which the risk profile for that list is being created and the likelihood of my fitting into it. My knowledge of this cannot be provided in advance without this undermining the predictive power of the profile. There is a deep tension here between this mode of governance and the idea that we are a community ruled by

---

[85] David Lyon & Kevin Haggerty, "The Surveillance Legacies of 9/11: Recalling, Reflecting on, and Rethinking Surveillance in the Security Era," *Canadian Journal of Law and Society* 27 (2013), 291.

law. This is something that requires much more reflection, but the traditional paradigms of privacy are likely not going to be as helpful as returning to our basic ideas of law.

Conclusions

In this chapter I have been arguing that consent-based privacy models are inadequate in the face of contemporary information practices and the emerging corporate–state nexus that has created such a striking surveillance infrastructure on the internet. Instead, in order to inspire a new approach I suggested that we focus on the idea of power, both in terms of power-over and power-to. Power-over connects privacy back to its rule-of-law roots from search and seizure law, but draws upon contemporary thinking about the rule of law for new resources for thinking through these informational issues. Power-to connects privacy to the facilitative role law plays, which is very clear when we look at legal powers. This helps us move away from a focus on privacy harms to a focus on what kind of legal norms can facilitate our social interactions. Power in this twin sense connects privacy to larger ideas of law and the ways in which law constitutes our world and our possibilities. In an information age that is somewhat chastened of late, this must be a good thing. If we are going to understand the ways in which power is configured, controlled, and harnessed in our information society then we need a broader legal canvass than simply the idea of privacy.

4

What's Wrong with Privacy Protections? Provocations from a Fifth Columnist

Kevin D. Haggerty

Introduction

Imagine you have travelled back in time to 1985 to tell North Americans about the future. You approach a group of astounded individuals and summarize for them the surveillance dynamics of our contemporary society, including widespread surveillance cameras, private and public organizations monitoring our communications, and corporations that track our travel and consumption patterns and trace our physical location in real time via our cell phones. Many in your audience, I suspect, will be incredulous, and will simply refuse to believe such things will happen. For them such a future seems impossible because their society recognizes privacy rights and has mechanisms to protect those rights. While correct about the existence of privacy laws, the fundamental issue these people are raising is the extent to which those laws meaningfully curtail the expansion of surveillance, which is the topic of this chapter.

Lawyers and regulators dominate discussions about privacy and privacy law. In contrast, I am a social scientist interested in the big picture, and what our current situation might suggest about larger social, political, and historical trends. My background is in Surveillance Studies, an interdisciplinary field that critically analyzes how surveillance operates in different realms.[1] I therefore bring to this discussion insights from someone who is not a complete insider to privacy's legal nuances, but who is attuned to the contours of contemporary debates about privacy's value and utility.

In what follows I make some sweeping, provisional, and doubtlessly controversial observations about privacy, specifically concerning how far privacy laws and data protection regimes are able to restrict surveillance, both today and into the future. It continues a discussion Professor Colin Bennett[2] initiated about the value of privacy as a concept and regulatory regime. Where Bennett shares with many

---

[1] Kirstie Ball, Kevin Haggerty, & David Lyon, *The Routledge Handbook of Surveillance Studies* (London: Routledge, 2012); David Lyon, *Surveillance Studies: An Overview* (Cambridge: Polity, 2007).

[2] Colin Bennett, "In Defence of Privacy: The Concept and the Regime," *Surveillance & Society* 8 (2011), 485.

practitioners a cautious commitment to the continuing utility of privacy, I am more despondent, and believe we should temper whatever remaining enthusiasm we might have about the possibility that privacy laws will effectively check the growth of surveillance.

I have facetiously characterized my comments as those of a "fifth columnist" – an expression used to denigrate individuals who work from within to undermine a group's activities. While I understand why some might see my observations in that light, my aim is not to undermine the value of privacy. In truth, I emphatically believe in the importance of a robust private realm. Consequently I am encouraging an unflinching assessment of whether our legal and administrative frameworks are up to the formidable task of impeding our headlong rush towards an ever-more expansive surveillance society.[3]

Surveillance involves collecting and analyzing information about populations and places for purposes of governance. Surveillance is therefore not confined to the familiar realms of cameras and spies, but entails all kinds of monitoring practices, themselves often based on an expanding range of technologies. Privacy and surveillance have a complicated relationship, but for the purpose of this chapter we will simply assume that privacy declines as surveillance expands to monitor more people in greater detail.

[3] Surveillance Studies Network, "A Report on the Surveillance Society," *UK Information Commissioner* (2006).

Many scholars have assessed whether privacy laws and regulations can counter specific surveillance practices. My overly ambitious aim is to ask if the laws designed to protect privacy, when looked at as a whole, offer realistic hope of insulating us from the powerful forces coalescing to reduce the reality of privacy.

Pundits have repeatedly pronounced privacy dead.[4] But even those authors typically do not believe privacy has been eliminated. They are simply trying to focus attention on unpalatable practices. My position, in contrast, is that it is empirically the case that privacy has been in consistent – but not linear or uniform – decline for over a century. The privacy infrastructure is proving ill equipped to check this accelerating process. To detail this situation I first accentuate my own approach to the reality of privacy (as distinct from the usual focus on privacy understood as legally delimited privacy violations) and why privacy must be protected. I then outline several factors limiting the efficacy of the privacy infrastructure, and detail how capitalism's portentous arrival on the privacy stage will likely challenge existing privacy protections. My concluding comments finesse my position in anticipation of criticisms I expect from those who will find my observations too sweeping, despairing, or even alarmist.

[4] Lori Andrews, *I Know Who You are and I Saw What You Did: Social Networks and the Death of Privacy* (New York: The Free Press, 2013); Simson Garfinkle, *Database Nation: The Death of Privacy in the 21st Century* (Sebastopol: O'Reilly, 2000).

The reality of privacy

Privacy is an example of what sociologist Emile Durkheim[5] referred to as a social fact. It is a thing in the world, a reality of individuals and groups, with legal, moral, institutional, and economic components. Most basically, privacy is a place (simultaneously spatial, psychological, and informational) where individuals are relatively free from interpersonal or institutional scrutiny.[6] Absolute privacy, however, does not exist. Or, more accurately, it may exist in some rare circumstances, but it requires extreme efforts to completely remove oneself from all social interaction, and as such is not typically desirable. Absolute privacy is also increasingly inconceivable as even the planet's most remote places are increasingly monitored.[7]

Privacy exists on a continuum. Individuals at different times and in different contexts have more or less privacy. This is a fairly standard and perhaps old-fashioned definition, but it has the advantage of not getting bogged down in the almost infinite number of contextual factors that shape someone's subjective assessment of whether something

---

[5] Emile Durkheim, "What Is a Social Fact?" in *The Rules of Sociological Method*, ed. George Catlin (New York: The Free Press, 1938).

[6] Ruth Gavison, "Privacy and the Limits of Law," *Yale Law Journal* 89 (1980), 421.

[7] Kevin Haggerty & Daniel Trottier, "Surveillance and/of Nature: Monitoring Beyond the Human," *Society and Animals* (2013).

infringes their personal sense of privacy.[8] Instead, the focus is on wholesale quantitative changes in the reality of privacy. Concentrating on the quantitative dimension allows us to foreground the degrees of privacy characteristic of different societies – a necessarily speculative exercise as there is no satisfactory way to calculate the sum total of privacy. Such assessments, however, need not be arbitrary, as careful attention to surveillance allows us to draw conclusions about whether one culture might have more or less privacy than another, and if the aggregate of privacy is increasing or decreasing.

Early humans, for example, apparently had little privacy. Locke[9] summarizes the anthropological and archeological evidence to paint a picture of nomadic peoples for whom privacy was not a meaningful phenomenon. Living in intimately small egalitarian groups, individuals were routinely visible to one another. Only approximately 12,000 years ago did humans begin a slow process of domestication as they haltingly moved from open living arrangements into permanent structures. The catalyst for this change appears to have been the growing size of human groups. Greater numbers spurred a desire to avoid the constant gaze of other people.

---

[8] Gary Marx, "Varieties of Personal Information as Influences on Attitudes Towards Surveillance," in *The New Politics of Surveillance and Visibility*, eds. Kevin D. Haggerty and Richard Ericson (Toronto: University of Toronto Press, 2006).

[9] John L. Locke, *Eavesdropping: An Intimate History* (Oxford: Oxford University Press, 2010).

It stimulated a corresponding yearning to escape the burdens of watching, of having to constantly assess the moods and intentions of an expanding number of people encountered face-to-face. Domestication produced qualitatively different forms of privacy, but more significantly – even monumentally – it expanded the amount of privacy. People could now retreat behind walls to avoid being watched, and get away from the exhausting need to constantly scrutinize an expanding number of people.

Characterizing privacy as a "reality" signals how my approach differs from the main orientations to privacy that typically start from a different set of assumptions, ambitions, and disciplinary traditions. For the most part lawyers and regulators now own the concept of privacy, something that profoundly shapes how it is understood. Serious discussions of privacy are often highly legalistic, and gloss over the question of what privacy actually is, and how much we might have or need. Such legal-centrism is apparent in Professor Richards' contribution to this volume, where he defines privacy as "the rules we have as a society for managing the collection, use, and disclosure of personal information."[10] This position confuses the rules for the thing itself – privacy – that the rules should protect. Comparable legal-centrism has resulted in a cottage industry of competing legal definitions of privacy violations.[11] While those definitions differ in their

[10] Neil M. Richards, "Four Privacy Myths," in Chapter 1 of this volume, p. 35.

[11] Daniel Solove, *Understanding Privacy* (Cambridge: Harvard University Press, 2008).

particulars, they all tend to accentuate information self-determination. This orientation seeks to protect a person's autonomous ability to control his or her personal information or access to their self, and requires organizations to inform people about when they are under surveillance and how their information is used.

My concern for the reality of privacy is fundamentally different from privacy framed as a legal violation. The hypothetical example of an extreme exhibitionist makes the difference abundantly clear. Our exhibitionist videotapes everything she does, surrenders all of her information online, publicizes her movements, and even freely shares her most intimate thoughts. Following almost all legal definitions of privacy this situation would not be a privacy violation, as she chooses to reveal her information. At the same time – *and this is the crucial point* – she would undeniably be experiencing a quantitative reduction in the reality of her privacy. The reality of privacy can be, and routinely is, reduced through developments lawyers would not recognize as actionable privacy violations.

Analysts have identified many complex normative, political, and personal implications of privacy. Among the more significant is how the historical emergence of privacy allowed individuals to forge identities distinct from the larger group.[12]

---

[12] Julie E. Cohen, "What Privacy Is For," *Harvard Law Review* 126 (2013), 1904–1933; John L. Locke, *Eavesdropping: An Intimate History* (Oxford: Oxford University Press).

Privacy ushered in a domestic realm – with different implications for men and women[13] – and is a precondition for
politics and dissent in complex modern societies. Privacy
also nurtured suspicions about what people were doing
behind closed doors, prompting a rise in interpersonal
eavesdropping and efforts to identify trustworthy individuals from the masses of people whose reputations could not
be personally verified.[14]

My focus here is on one particularly vital, although often
underestimated, attribute of privacy. Privacy is a check on
organizational manipulation and authoritarian forms of
rule. When individuals are secure in a realm where they
are comparatively unknown by large organizations this ham-
pers the possibilities for the development of authoritarian
forms of government and social control that are latent in all
modern societies.[15] While lawyers typically focus on privacy
violations – and I unreservedly share those concerns – I also
worry about the broader political and social implications of a
decline in the reality of privacy, as it is, in part, this ability to
remain unknown, untracked, and unseen that insulates people from the extremes of institutional manipulation, coercion, and repression.

---

[13] Anita Allen, *Uneasy Access: Privacy for Women in a Free Society*
(New York: Rowman and Littlefield, 1988).

[14] Steven L. Nock, *The Costs of Privacy: Surveillance and Reputation in
America* (New York: Aldine de Gruyter, 1993).

[15] Zygmunt Bauman, *Modernity and the Holocaust* (New York: Cornell
University Press, 1989).

So my concern is not solely with the reduction of privacy. Instead, I worry about what privacy's decline has empowered. Privacy is not being diminished by a rejuvenation of the face-to-face intimacies of early modern life. Instead, the loss of privacy is matched by a corresponding and unprecedented intensification in institutions' informational capacities.[16] Such a situation carries with it stark prospects for repressive forms of control, as surveillance is a key power resource in all forms of totalitarianism. As Anthony Giddens puts it, "The possibilities of totalitarian rule depend upon the existence of societies in which the state can successfully penetrate the day-to-day activities of most of its subject populations."[17] History has demonstrated how such repression becomes easier when privacy is reduced by even small increases in organizational information processing capabilities.[18] Such surveillance resources have never been more powerful or accessible.

We therefore have two quite different ways of thinking about the privacy situation. Lawyers, administrators, and many activists tend to focus on legally circumscribed and actionable privacy infringements that produce immediate,

[16] David Lyon, *Surveillance Studies: An Overview* (Cambridge: Polity, 2007); Arnand Mattelart, *The Globalization of Surveillance*. Trans. Susan Taponier & James A. Cohen (London: Polity, 2010).

[17] Anthony Giddens, *The Nation-State and Violence* (Cambridge: Polity, 1987), 302.

[18] Edwin Black, *IBM and the Holocaust: The Strategic Alliance Between Nazi Germany and America's Most Powerful Corporation* (New York: Crown Publishers, 2001).

identifiable, and concrete harms to individuals (and sometimes to groups). My orientation, in contrast, is to the societal-
wide risks inherent in reduced privacy, something that does
not in itself necessarily result in easily identifiable immediate
harms, but increases the prospect of manipulative or coercive
forms of social control. Such concerns explain why I use the
privacy regimes' ability to protect the reality of privacy as a
benchmark to evaluate its successes and limitations.

The successes and limits of privacy

While privacy entails being relatively free from scrutiny, it
now has several other facets. Looked at from different
angles, privacy has had tremendous institutional and cultural successes.

Discursively, privacy is a clear winner. It is our main
conceptual resource for critiquing any potentially negative
implications of surveillance and information systems. People
now invoke it almost mechanically in such debates. Privacy is
so hegemonic it is impossible to imagine what could replace it
on the political stage. At the institutional level entire organizations have mandates to protect privacy. Individuals craft
careers as privacy commissioners, privacy officers, activists,
and lawyers,[19] producing a privacy infrastructure replete
with dedicated conferences, websites, and journals. The

[19] Colin Bennett, The *Privacy Advocates: Resisting the Spread of
Surveillance* (Cambridge, MA: MIT, 2008).

privacy infrastructure's expansion loosely mirrors (but on a much smaller scale) the growth in surveillance and increased risks that such monitoring poses to basic freedoms.

The emergence of careers in the privacy infrastructure, combined with privacy law becoming entrenched in legal education and professional practice, has resulted in a tsunami of publications on the topic. As one small illustration, a search on Google Scholar for articles with "privacy" in the title for just the year 2012 returns 4,350 separate pieces. This compares to 469 articles containing the word "tort" in the title for the same year and 2,080 with "copyright" in the title – at a time when copyright was a major political issue globally.

There have never been more privacy laws, a richer professional discourse on the topic, or a more extensive and dedicated network of privacy professionals. One might therefore anticipate a correspondingly large and well-preserved private sphere. Just the opposite is the case. Over the course of many decades surveillance has expanded and intensified almost everywhere, becoming a dominant organizational practice.[20]

This extraordinary surveillance growth stands as one of the most singular facts of our day. It is transforming how we shop, find our partners, produce goods, educate our children, fight wars, govern, deliver healthcare, and almost every other facet of human existence. The expansion and intensification

---

[20] The New Transparency Project. *Transparent Lives: Surveillance in Canada* (Atabasca: Athabasca University Press, 2014).

of surveillance is also a blunt indictment of the efficacy of the privacy infrastructure, the value of which, for me, hinges to a significant extent on its ability to effectively restrict surveillance.

The literature now overflows with reasons to be skeptical of the ability of privacy regimes to curtail surveillance. Some of these factors are set out below, followed by discussion of how emerging corporate imperatives to acquire personal data and market surveillance products should give us even greater reason to contemplate how privacy will be qualitatively transformed, and quantitatively curtailed, in the coming years.

The United States differs from other Western nations in not having governmental bodies mandated to protect privacy. Nothing in the United States compares, for example, to Canada's network of privacy commissions. Instead, Americans concerned about privacy often have few official options other than to turn to the courts. A number of familiar criticisms of the legal system are therefore acute concerns for privacy advocates. The courts are conservative, and slow-acting. By the time cases are adjudicated on the privacy invasive attributes of particular technologies, those devices have often become firmly entrenched in institutional practice and citizens have become accustomed to their existence.

Most citizens simply cannot afford to use the courts. Powerful institutional actors, in contrast, have time and again demonstrated they are well positioned to advance their interests through the legal system. This is a serious concern for privacy advocates given how the forces supporting greater surveillance are often the state and major corporations.

Organizations and individuals have starkly differential abilities to capitalize on privacy protections. For example, we recently witnessed the galling spectacle of the Inspector General of the Office of the US Director of National Intelligence refusing to reveal how many Americans had their privacy violated through warrantless wiretap provisions because he claimed releasing this information would violate those individual's privacy rights.[21] Or, as Richards points out in his contribution to this volume, Facebook uses non-disclosure agreements to effectively censor what researchers and journalists can say about that company's operations[22]. What is maddening about these situations is they involve organizations whose *modus operandi* is to collect massive amounts of personal information. So as social inequality and differential power make it effectively impossible for individual citizens to enforce their privacy rights,[23] data collectors deploy their wealth and legal acumen to hide their actions behind privacy protections.

For those cases that actually do make it to court, privacy litigation in the United States often revolves around the twin

[21] Spencer Ackerman, "NSA: It Would Violate Your Privacy to Say if We Spied on You," *Wired* (June 18, 2012), available at http://www.wired.com/dangerroom/2012/06/nsa-spied.

[22] Neil M. Richards, "Four Privacy Myths," in Chapter 1 of this volume, p. 46.

[23] John Gilliom, *Overseers of the Poor: Surveillance, Resistance, and the Limits of Privacy* (Chicago: University of Chicago Press, 2001).

issues of consent and notice. I address consent in the later discussion of informational capitalism. The notice criterion essentially holds that privacy expectations can, at times, be overwritten if the monitoring agents make people aware of such scrutiny. The logic here is that individuals can avoid institutional scrutiny if informed of where and when it exists. The limitations of such an approach are starkly apparent given how life's necessities are now secured through institutions that regularly require individuals to surrender personal information as a precondition for accessing resources and services.[24]

The defects of notice as a means to protect privacy can be seen, for example, in relation to surveillance cameras. Such cameras have expanded almost everywhere over the past twenty years, but perhaps nowhere more than in the United Kingdom[25] where they have produced a corresponding urban blight of inescapable signs announcing the pervasive presence of cameras. Individuals are informed they are being watched, but have little prospect of avoiding camera scrutiny. The aesthetics of England's cities would be drastically improved if all those signs were replaced with a handful identifying the few places not watched by cameras. Notice, here as elsewhere, has proved to be entirely compatible with the expansion and intensification of surveillance.

---

[24] Michalis Lianos, *The New Social Control* (Ottawa: Red Quill, 2012).

[25] Clive Norris & Gary Armstrong, *The Maximum Surveillance Society: The Rise of CCTV* (Oxford: Berg, 1999).

The US Supreme Court recognizes the need to protect the public's reasonable privacy expectations, which is undoubtedly a good thing. Further prodding, however, suggests that having privacy rest on "public expectations" paradoxically introduces an inclination towards greater surveillance into the heart of privacy law. While the court reserves for itself almost absolute discretion to determine the public's privacy expectations, the fact those expectations change in relation to personal experiences is reason for concern. As surveillance becomes an ever-more routine aspect of our lives the public's privacy expectations appear to be declining, and the courts will undoubtedly appeal to this tendency to justify further limitations on privacy.

Privacy is a "parenthood" issue. Citizens and the judiciary both support privacy in the abstract. Such support, however, is consistently challenged by how privacy is routinely in tension with other desirable values we, as a society, seek to advance. Moving from endorsing abstract sentiments to the *realpolitik* of actually protecting privacy can involve placing limits on such elements as bureaucratic efficiency, economic competition, or personal security that are unpopular among some constituencies.

One right being in tension with another is not unique to privacy. More disconcerting is the demonstrated trend whereby the courts and individual citizens see privacy concerns as less pressing or pivotal than national security, international competitiveness, or other issues. Ultimately, Cohen concludes that "privacy comes up the loser" when it "must be balanced against the cutting-edge imperatives of national security, efficiency, and entrepreneurship."[26] The risks of reduced privacy can appear esoteric and hypothetical when compared to other needs – limitations that are always easier to frame as being more pressing and weighty.

Officials regularly portray security as being in tension or even incompatible with privacy.[27] Since the 9/11 terrorist attacks, officials have repeatedly invoked security concerns to expand the scope of the state's policing and security surveillance infrastructure.[28] Rather than being able to watch the privacy establishment effectively marshal privacy laws to check such efforts, attentive citizens have instead learned about the broad legislative exemptions allowing for surveillance justified as a national security measure.

No one wants to *meaningfully* increase the *realistic* risks of *serious* terrorist attacks. But officials now routinely, and often cynically, frame myriad political issues as security concerns to advance legislative ambitions and insulate policy from criticism[29] – a process sociologists refer to as "securitization."

[26] Julie E. Cohen, "What Privacy Is For," *Harvard Law Review* 126 (2013), 1904.

[27] Daniel Solove, *Nothing to Hide: The False Tradeoff Between Privacy and Security* (New Haven: Yale University Press, 2011).

[28] David Lyon, *Surveillance After September 11* (London: Polity, 2003).

[29] Mark Neocleous, "Against Security," *Radical Philosophy* 100 (2000), 7; John Mueller, *Overblown: How Politicians and the Terrorism Industry Inflate National Security Threats, and Why We Believe Them* (New York: The Free Press, 2006).

Privacy laws' broad security exemptions make it difficult for concerned citizens to identify even the broad contours of how surveillance operates in the aid of national security and whether such measures are successful, cost effective, or excessively invasive.[30] This is a crucial limitation given how, on those rare occasions when political controversies have lifted the veil of secrecy on such surveillance, we have repeatedly seen how officials use national secrecy exemptions to avoid political embarrassment and mask violations of process and abuses of power.[31]

One final difficulty with relying upon the courts to curtail surveillance is that courts will not restrict a surveillance measure unless they conclude that this practice infringes an identifiable right. This is a comparatively high bar, meaning a litany of surveillance practices cumulatively falling below that threshold – but which nonetheless reduce the reality of privacy – are never litigated or are deemed to not violate privacy rights. As such, the legal emphasis on privacy violations contributes to the ongoing decline of privacy not necessarily through a one-time massive incursion (although such things occasionally happen) but by positioning a series

[30] Sunny Hughes, "US Domestic Surveillance After 9/11: An Analysis of the Chilling Effect on First Amendment Rights in Cases Filed Against the Terrorist Surveillance Program," *Canadian Journal of Law and Society* 27 (2012), 399.

[31] Colin Freeze, "Canada's Spy Agencies Chastised for Duping Courts," *The Globe and Mail* (December 20, 2013).

of curtailments below the threshold of legal recognition and enforcement.

Despite the courts' obvious problems, Americans should be careful about envying other countries' privacy institutions. Canada's network of privacy commissioners, for example, has checked some egregious surveillance measures but its ability to pursue such cases, and effectively curtail such behaviors, are severely constrained. Remember, it was a Canadian privacy commissioner who decided a sports facility was not violating privacy regulations when it installed surveillance cameras in the men's changing rooms, as the facility restricted what was recorded and who could see the images.[32] This is, therefore, a privacy infrastructure that accommodates something as iconically invasive as cameras in changing rooms.

Commissioners tend to be seriously underfunded and are straddled with the contradictory directive to both protect privacy and ensure people and organizations can access information. Canada's flagship national privacy legislation, for example, is the Freedom of Information and Protection of Privacy Act – and its title gives a sense of the somewhat schizophrenic mandate of privacy commissioners who, while having some scope for proactive advocacy, cannot initiate cases and must wait for citizens to come to them with complaints. Commissioners can determine individuals or organizations are violating privacy laws, but have no power

---

[32] Alberta Office of the Information and Privacy Commissioner, Order P2006–008, March 14, 2007, Lindsay Park Sports Facility.

(beyond moral suasion and public shaming) to enforce their judgments.

Privacy commissioners find themselves in delicate political situations because they are ultimately beholden to the same governments whose actions they are often trying to curtail. An example from the Canadian province of Alberta is illustrative. Several years ago Alberta's privacy commissioner investigated several nightclubs because security staff were scanning patrons' personal information from their driver's licenses or other official forms of identification before those clients were allowed to enter.[33] That personal information was then stored on private computers. The privacy commissioner ruled this violated the province's Personal Information Privacy Act. The provincial government's response was to simply amend the Gaming and Liquor Act to allow this information to be collected, notwithstanding the fact such collection violated basic privacy principles.

Privacy commissioners oversee regulations oriented to widely accepted "fair information practices" for collecting and processing personal data. These include the expectation that organizations maintaining data on people must be accountable for all the personal information they possess, should identify the purposes for which the information is collected at or before the time of collection, should retain information only as long as required, should only collect the

---

[33] Kevin D. Haggerty & Camille Tokar, "Signifying Security: On the Institutional Appeals of Nightclub ID Scanning Systems," *Space & Culture* 15 (2012), 124.

personal information necessary for pursuing the identified purpose, and should only collect personal information with the knowledge and consent of the individual.[34]

Such principles are reassuring, but closer scrutiny suggests this legal framework actually enables massive data collection. This is because the fair information practices are primarily procedural. As such they do not address what James Rule characterizes as "the most important of all surveillance issues ... [w]hen is it reasonable to judge that specific forms of it simply *go too far*, even in the service of the most estimable social purpose."[35] The principles amount to a series of not particularly onerous benchmarks organizations must meet in order to have their data collection efforts officially sanctioned. Consequently, fair information practices produce a more fair system of information use and management (i.e., they meet procedural standards) but, as Bennett notes, they "cannot control the voracious and inherent appetite of modern organizations for more and more increasingly refined personal information."[36]

But it is not simply that such regulations cannot stop the rampant collection of information; the due process orientation

---

[34] Colin Bennett & Charles Raab, *The Governance of Privacy: Policy Instruments in Global Perspective* (Aldershot: Ashgate, 2003).

[35] James B. Rule, "The Movement to Protect Privacy," in *Routledge Handbook of Surveillance Studies*, eds. Kevin D. Haggerty, Kirstie Ball, and David Lyon (London: Routledge, 2013), 69 (original emphasis).

[36] Colin Bennett, "In Defence of Privacy: The Concept and the Regime," *Surveillance & Society* 8 (2011), 485.

can actually empower institutions to conduct surveillance and reduce privacy. To appreciate this situation we can make a useful analogy with traffic regulations. Traffic rules pertaining to signage, licensing, weight restrictions, speed limits, and the like, are not intended to seriously curtail vehicular traffic. Instead, they prohibit behaviors at the margins in the hope of producing an efficient system of motorized transportation – which nonetheless sometimes results in gridlock.

Something like this is happening with privacy regulations. These rules constrain some excesses in the hope of establishing an efficient, predictable, and procedurally fair system of data collection. This is apparent, for example, in how Canadian Privacy Commissions have worked with industry to develop guidelines for privately operated surveillance cameras.[37] While restricting egregious misuse, such as using cameras to peer into the windows of businesses or residences, the camera guidelines' focus on signage amounts to a low regulatory standard that has facilitated the diffusion of cameras across Canadian cities.[38] In this situation "privacy is becoming less a barrier to governmental

---

[37] Office of the Privacy Commissioner of Canada (OPCC), Office of the Information and Privacy Commissioner of Alberta (OIPCA), Officer of the Information and Privacy Commissioner of British Columbia (OIPCBC), 2008. Mar.). Guidelines for Overt Video Surveillance in the Private Sector. Retrieved from http://www.oipc.bc.ca/news/rlsgen/Video_Surveillance_Guidelines%28March2008%29.pdf

[38] Sean Hier, *Panoptic Dreams: Streetscape Video Surveillance in Canada* (Vancouver: UBC Press, 2010).

power and more an instrument of its exercise."[39] Professor Austin's contribution to this volume makes a comparable point about how Canadian Privacy Commissions have legitimated Facebook's data collection model and supported state efforts to access customer information collected by internet service providers (ISPs), concluding that in such instances privacy can "work to enable surveillance."[40]

All of this combines with the disconcerting tendency for organizations to flout privacy laws, or develop ingenious legal "work-arounds" to keep their actions within the letter of the law while violating its intent. Three examples drawn from different realms will provide a sense of this situation.

> The first one relates to the national "do not call" registries that allow citizens to indicate they do not want unsolicited marketing calls in both Canada and the United States. Widely supported, the registries were initially hailed as a victory for privacy – although they are a political compromise falling far below actually banning such calls. But even this half measure is now routinely contravened by a telephone spamming industry willing to simply ignore the law, with few discernible consequences.[41]

[39] Randy Lippert & Kevin Walby, "Governing Through Privacy: Authoritarian Liberalism, Law, and Privacy Knowledge," *Law, Culture and the Humanities* (forthcoming), 1.

[40] Lisa Austin, "Enough About Me: Why Privacy is About Power, Not Consent," in Chapter 3 of this volume.

[41] Jim Handy, "Does the 'Do Not Call' List Even Work?" *Forbes* (December 17, 2013), available at http://www.forbes.com/sites/jim handy/2013/02/27/does-the-do-not-call-list-even-work.

The second example concerns the "fusion centers" run jointly by US Homeland Security and the Department of Justice. In keeping with the spirit of our era, fusion centers have a mandate to collect, analyze, and share as much terrorism-relevant information (extremely broadly defined) as possible between federal, state, and private agencies. Fusion centers have now significantly expanded their focus beyond terrorism to encompass detecting and preventing all crimes, hazards, and threats. Government officials responsible for fusion centers have repeatedly proclaimed their support for privacy, but their entire organizational structure appears designed to reside in law's interstitial spaces, severely complicating oversight and accountability. Fusion centers are repeatedly criticized for conducting illegal informational "fishing expeditions," violating legal requirements that citizens only be investigated under conditions where there is reasonable suspicion to believe they are involved in criminal activity. Rather than strictly abiding by privacy laws, Citron and Pasquale[42] characterize the legal situation of fusion centers as a process of "regulatory arbitrage" where actors strategically capitalize on the abundant opportunities to shift their activities to the least stringent regulatory regime.

The final example concerns the previously mentioned surveillance camera guidelines crafted by Canadian privacy

---

[42] Danielle Keats Citron & Frank Pasquale, "Network Accountability for the Domestic Intelligence Apparatus," *Hastings Law Journal* 62 (2011), 141.

commissioners in consultation with business interests. Those regulations emphasize appropriate signage. Camera operators are supposed to post visible, legible signs identifying the camera's owner, the purposes for the data collection, and contact details. In 2011 Professor Clement conducted a study of 300 retail establishments in downtown Toronto. He found roughly 60 percent had no visible sign alerting people to the camera's presence.[43] Not one sign met the guidelines' minimum requirements.

I could outline more of the limitations on the privacy establishment now identified in the voluminous privacy literature. Remember, however, that these are all broad trends, so it is not the case, for example, that security will always trump privacy, or that privacy advocates' victories will inevitably be undermined by organizations willing to work around or flout privacy regulations. But compiling even a partial inventory of such limitations suggests a dominant pattern.

The dominant trajectory

For over a century privacy has been declining in Western societies as surveillance capacity increases. Figure 2 crudely represents this situation. But it does not just portray privacy receding over time, it depicts a staggered decline. Reductions

---

[43] Jeff Gray, "Toronto's CCTV Cameras: Who is Watching the Watchers," *Globe and Mail* (May 13, 2011).

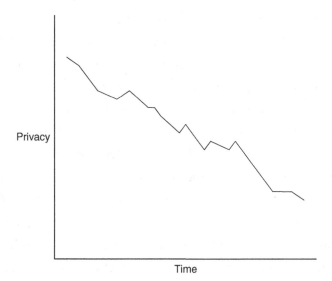

Figure 2 The cumulative decline of privacy

in privacy have been consistent but erratic. At different times important developments in, for example, information technology, have helped reduce privacy, while at other times the privacy infrastructure has won notable victories, producing an uptick in privacy. Sometimes privacy has stayed somewhat stable during periods of comparative lull, as was probably the case in the years after the spying scandals of the COINTELPRO era (1956 to 1971) when the FBI was compelled to curtail its covert surveillance of civil rights, antiwar, and political groups.[44]

Imagine a recurring procession of surveillance surges, each starting with an attempt to increase surveillance

[44] Gary T. Marx, *Undercover: Police Surveillance in America* (Berkeley: University of California Press, 1988).

capacity. A surveillance surge might involve a single piece of legislation, organizational practice, or technology that increases the legibility of a subset of the population. Sometimes surges are starkly apparent, as occurred after 9/11 when a plethora of surveillance measures were deployed in an attempt to thwart terrorism.[45] In fact, the situation immediately after 9/11 involved a major surge comprising a series of more minor surges, each modifying existing laws or introducing new information technologies. After the onset of each surge the courts and administrative bodies eventually addressed the legality of the surveillance practice, rendering decisions that curtailed some excesses (framed as privacy violations), but did not quite return the situation to that which preceded the surge.

So surveillance capacity expands, is beaten back slightly (occasionally considerably) by the courts and administrative structures, but leaves behind a residuum of greater surveillance than existed initially. In this way the harshest surveillance measures are curtailed, but a net increase in surveillance is still the result. As this happens thousands of times over the course of decades the process cumulatively

---

[45] Kevin D. Haggerty & Amber Gazso, "Seeing Beyond the Ruins: Surveillance as a Response to Terrorist Threats," *Canadian Journal of Sociology* 30 (2005), 169; Reg. Whitaker, "A Faustian Bargain: America and the Dream of Total Information Awareness," in *The New Politics of Surveillance and Visibility*, eds. Kevin D. Haggerty & Richard V. Ericson (Toronto: University of Toronto Press, 2006).

slides towards reducing privacy, even as egregious privacy violations are reigned in.

This surge process should not be confused with the popular "pendulum" theory of civil liberties that suggests in times of crisis legislators embrace (or tolerate) measures that swing the legal pendulum towards constricting human rights. Over time, however, as the situation normalizes, the courts check these legal excesses, and the pendulum swings back to its original position.[46] The surge process is different because it is not exclusively concerned with civil rights, but with the introduction of surveillance more generally. And where the pendulum theory expects the rights pendulum to eventually return to its starting point, the image of a surge accentuates how even when the excesses of surveillance measures are moderated, over time what remains is a situation of greater surveillance than at the outset – sometimes much greater, and at other times only moderately so.

Relying on privacy laws to protect the reality of privacy resembles the situation of the gambler whose lifelong strategy is to bet against the house. She will have some wins, but over the long term her losses are preordained because the odds have been purposely set against her. In the privacy realm the long odds are not necessarily intentionally set against privacy advocates – although that is sometimes the

---

[46] Eric Posner & Adrien Vermeule, *Terror in the Balance: Security, Liberty and the Courts* (Oxford: Oxford University Press, 2007).

legislators' clear design. Instead, this disadvantageous situation is usually the cumulative result of the types of system limitations identified above. And now a comparatively new player has stepped up to the table, promising to even further stack the deck against privacy.

Informational capitalism and surveillance markets

Corporations have ominously appeared on the privacy stage. Developments in informational capitalism and the growth of a lucrative market for surveillance products promise to further constrict the reality of privacy. We can predict the informational needs of capitalism, combined with the influence of the surveillance industrial complex, will strain, or perhaps overwhelm, established privacy protections.

Organizations have always collected and used data.[47] But a new form of informational capitalism is being entrenched in Western nations, one that depends on radically enhanced corporate abilities to acquire, manipulate, and sell personal information.[48] Informational capitalism – which involves a hybrid of state and corporate actors – presents some unfamiliar challenges to activists who have

---

[47] Christopher Dandeker, *Surveillance, Power and Modernity: Bureaucracy and Discipline from 1700 to the Present Day* (New York: St. Martin's, 1990).

[48] Manuel Castells, *The Rise of the Network Society* (Oxford: Blackwell, 1996); Dan Schiller, *How to Think About Information* (Urbana: University of Illinois Press, 2007).

long been primarily attuned to the privacy risks posed by the state. While state power remains a concern, we also need to pay greater attention to how capitalist interests are coalescing to undermine privacy, and contemplate whether privacy protections can meaningfully constrain capital's escalating informational demands.

Only recently have we started to appreciate the enormity of the threat informational capitalism poses to our privacy protections. This is most apparent in debates about "big data,"[49] which refers to organizational efforts to capitalize on new abilities to identify patterns in massive stores of personal data. The aim is to use supercomputers to mine the information now available to organizations in search of otherwise invisible connections between people and processes.

While big data advocates are guilty of hyping its revolutionary potential, there is no denying that something monumental is occurring in the budding organizational quest for the surplus value concealed in personal data warehouses. The insights produced by big data promise to enhance healthcare, rationalize transit, and produce greater profit margins, among many other things. But all such benefits hinge on institutions securing greater access to personal information and reducing legal encumbrances on their abilities to manipulate those data.

---

[49] Omer Tene & Jules Polonetsky, "Privacy in the Age of Big Data: A Time for Big Decisions," *Stanford Law Review* 64 (2012), 63.

Big data advocates' ambitions are sometimes in tension with privacy laws and fair information practices. It will be intriguing to see how long this situation lasts before the regulations are brought into line with corporate interests. To fully recognize the threat posed to privacy by an ascendant form of capitalism based on unfettered access to personal data, we need to appreciate that legal rights can decline and sometimes disappear entirely. Historically, the drive to accommodate the needs of capital has played a role in diminishing certain rights.

A useful analogy can be made with the enclosures movement that occurred over many centuries in Europe, peaking in England between 1760 and 1820.[50] Commoners then exercised longstanding – and legally recognized and protected – usufructuary rights. Such rights allowed them to "graze stock, cut wood or peat, draw water or grow crops, on various plots of land at specified times of year."[51] Usufructuary rights conflicted with an emerging industrial capitalism based on the private ownership of land – a comparatively new development at the time. Over many decades those rights were effectively ignored, swept away, and overwritten, in a process that helped establish the legal and material conditions for

[50] J. M. Neeson, *Commoners: Common Right, Enclosure, and Social Change in England, 1700–1820* (Cambridge: Cambridge University Press, 1993).

[51] Peter Linebaugh, "Enclosures from the Bottom Up," *Radical History Review* 108 (2010), 11.

industrial capitalism, with often disastrous consequences for the commoners' way of life. E. P. Thompson[52] famously characterized the enclosures as "a plain enough case of class robbery," and it was a robbery effected through, and legitimized by, the courts.

The point is that when longstanding rights impede capitalist access to a new material basis of production, those rights risk being overwritten. Admittedly such situations occur rarely, and any such result is not preordained. But I am suggesting we are on the cusp of a roughly analogous situation, as established privacy rights and fair information practices now somewhat limit how organizations access and use certain forms of data. Reforming such laws so that they better accord with the needs of informational capitalism will undoubtedly be a drawn-out process occurring over many decades. But organizations are already developing ingenious strategies to reduce or undermine legal privacy protections in efforts to obtain and manipulate personal data. Three recent examples give a sense of this situation.

The first concerns the limitations fair information practices place on what data can be collected, as organizations are expected to identify in advance how such data will be used. In the big-data world such restrictions are problematic because agencies want to use data not just for prospectively identifiable purposes, but to churn data to find unpredicted

[52] E. P. Thompson, *The Making of the English Working Class* (Harmondsworth: Penguin, 1963): 237.

insights. "With big data, the value of information no longer resides solely in its primary purpose ... it is now in secondary uses".[53] Consequently, corporations are lobbying to change existing privacy protection to "focus more on how data might be used rather than limit which data can be collected,"[54] something that would blunt a central fair information practice.

The second is a telling example of how one right can be portrayed as contravening another right, as organizations have sought to characterize privacy restrictions on how they use the information they collect as being contrary to the freedom of expression. A recent decision[55] by the Supreme Court of Canada hinged on this issue, with the court concluding the definition of personal information in the province of Alberta's Personal Information Protection Act (PIPA) was guilty of being too broad, and ignoring how organizations have an expressive interest in the information they collect. It criticized the provincial law for not having exemptions to allow organizations to use personal information in ways reasonably required in the legitimate operation of their businesses –

---

[53] Viktor Mayer-Schönberger & Kenneth Cukier, *Big Data: The Revolution That Will Transform How We Live, Work, and Think* (Boston: Houghton Mifflin Harcourt, 2013), 153.

[54] Joseph W. Jerome, "Buying and Selling Privacy: Big Data's Different Burdens and Its Benefits," *Stanford Law Review* 66 (2013), 47.

[55] *Alberta (Information and Privacy Commissioner) v. United Food and Commercial Workers*, Local 401, 2013 SCC 62.

without clarifying what might be included amongst such reasonable uses.

The decision strikes at the heart of existing understandings of personal information as enshrined in almost all fair data practices. It is so sweeping the court agreed with a request from the Information and Privacy Commissioner of Alberta and the Alberta Attorney General to strike down PIPA in its entirety, rather than try to craft a judicial compromise. The court gave the province one year to completely rework the legislation to bring it into line with their decision. And while corporations have long argued that privacy laws restrict corporate expression, this case was actually brought by a labor union. We can expect, however, that corporations will jump into the breach opened by this decision to dramatically expand how they use the information they collect.

The final example concerns corporate efforts to entice people to "voluntarily" surrender their information.[56] This practice hinges on a distinctive legal understanding of "consent" enshrined in privacy law and fair information practices that empowers organizations to collect and use personal information, providing individuals agree to such uses. Consent expectations are based on a form of privacy

---

[56] Jason Pridmore, "Consumer Surveillance: Context, Perspectives and Concerns in the Personal Information Economy," in *Routledge Handbook of Surveillance Studies*, eds. Kirstie Ball, Kevin D. Haggerty, & David Lyon (London: Routledge, 2012), 321.

self-management characteristic of liberal understandings of individual autonomy, but as Solove concludes, "does not provide people with meaningful control over their data."[57] In fact, how "consent" operates in practice is perhaps the biggest charade in privacy law. Rather than constrain information collection, consent has become a vehicle to sanction it.

Organizations use a litany of procedures to entice individuals to provide them spurious consent to acquire and use their personal data. This includes the rote requirements to click "agree" buttons in situations where people have little understanding of what they are agreeing to, nor any meaningful opportunity to opt out and still receive the desired service. Some organizations provide financial incentives at precisely calibrated thresholds designed to subtly entice people to surrender the maximum amount of information for the minimum return. Loyalty programs were early leaders in this area, giving registered customers discounts that in practice amount to punitive pricing schemes designed to encourage still more people to surrender their personal data. In exchange for their personal information individuals also sometimes receive easier or quicker access to certain services or locations. Looking to the near horizon, new organizational abilities to directly monitor such things as our health, physical location, or driving patterns by placing sensors in our

[57] Daniel Solove, "Privacy Self-Management and the Consent Dilemma," *Harvard Law Review* 126 (2013), 1880.

homes, cars, or on our bodies promise to intensify this process, as people will be given even more incentives to directly surrender information about the tiniest details of their lives.[58]

Advocates for big data repeatedly claim that personal data have become a vital natural resource; data are the "oil of the information economy."[59] This constant reference to personal data as a natural resource should be an eye-opener for privacy advocates given our failure to protect other natural resources from expropriation.

The corporate influence on privacy, however, extends beyond informational capitalism's thirst for personal information. Corporations have fully committed to developing and marketing surveillance products to some of the highest levels of government, both domestically and internationally. This process was underway before 9/11, but those attacks accelerated the sense that surveillance devices could address a range of problems both in security and other realms.

The result has been a growing surveillance industrial complex[60] involving close relationships between government

[58] Scott Peppett, "Unravelling Privacy: The Personal Prospectus & the Threat of a Full Disclosure Future," *Northwestern University Law Review* 105 (2011), 1153.

[59] Viktor Mayer-Schönberger & Kenneth Cukier, *Big Data: The Revolution That Will Transform How We Live, Work, and Think*, 16.

[60] ACLU, *Surveillance Industrial Complex* (New York, 2004); Ben Hayes, "'Full Spectrum Dominance' as European Union Security Policy: On the Trail of the 'NeoConOpticon'," in *Surveillance and Democracy*, eds. Kevin D. Haggerty and Minas Samatas (London:

officials and corporate lobbyists eager to secure lucrative government contracts for their surveillance devices. This symbiotic relationship maximizes profits while expanding the circuits of social control, reducing the reality of privacy in the process.

Where the surveillance industry was traditionally a comparatively small corner of the marketplace, Privacy International estimates the global trade in surveillance technology is now worth up to US$ 5 billion a year, which compares to the US$ 4 billion a year market in small arms.[61] Recent WikiLeaks documents demonstrate the surveillance products sold by these companies are some of the most sophisticated technologies available – including intrusion software, data mining, Trojans, location tracking, deep packet inspection, facial recognition, and mass monitoring.

In such a situation considerations about employing surveillance products become increasingly driven by corporate needs to find markets for their products. Organizations adopt such devices as a way to advance assorted agendas – including institutional desires to enhance their authority and display their modernity by deploying the latest high-tech gadgetry – rather than on a balanced assessment of benefits and risks.

Routledge, 2010), 148; Kirstie Ball & Laureen Snider, *The Surveillance-Industiral Complex: A Political Economy of Information* (London: Routledge, 2013).

[61] See http://wikileakssupportersforum.com/thread-600.html.

Discussion

Individuals working within the privacy infrastructure tend to be smart, committed, and politically savvy. I suspect many of these people will be perturbed by my three-part claim that: a) the privacy infrastructure has not been particularly successful over the long term in curtailing the expansion of surveillance, b) regulations justified as a way to protect privacy can help expand surveillance, and c) developments in information capitalism threaten to drastically reconfigure, or even overwhelm, privacy protections in the coming years. Indeed, I anticipate those who have spent their lives fine-tuning the privacy infrastructure will find my claims wrong-headed and impertinent. Such individuals will critique my position in some foreseeable ways I address here by way of a concluding discussion.

The most consequential criticism would be that, contrary to how I portray the situation, privacy has not been in long-term decline, but has remained stable or perhaps even increased. This goes to the heart of my position. It is also a difficult criticism to fully answer, given we cannot measure the quantity of privacy. Ultimately, my assessment is based on years of closely watching developments in surveillance. If others can look at this situation and conclude the private realm has not shrunk, I can only suggest we are in an incommensurable situation, one where we see the same things but perceive them in entirely incompatible ways.

The decline of privacy is all around us, but it is paradoxically hard to see. It is there in the more than 500 terabytes of personal data pouring into Facebook's databases every day (the entire holdings of the US Library of Congress amounts to a "mere" 10 terabytes of information).[62] It is in the 1.7 billion emails, phone calls, and other communications data the US National Security Agency (NSA) collects daily.[63] It is in the NSA's new data center that will be able to store one hundred years' worth of worldwide data communication.[64] It exists in the surveillance cameras authorities are now transforming into audio recorders and biometric identification devices.[65] It can be seen in the police's record 3 million unique searches (approximately 1 percent of the US population) on the US National Crime Information Center (NCIC) database in a single day in 2002.[66] It is in the drones that monitor our remote adversaries and national borders, and that will soon watch over

[62] Eliza Kern, Facebook is Collecting Your Data – 500 Terabytes a Day, *Gigaom* (December 27, 2013), available at http://gigaom.com/2012/08/22/facebook-is-collecting-your-data-500-terabytes-a-day.

[63] Dana Priest & William Arkin, "Top Secret America," *Washington Post* (July 19, 2010).

[64] Howard Berkes, "Amid Data Controversy, NSA Builds its Biggest Data Farm," *NPR* (February 13, 2014), http://www.npr.org/2013/06/10/190160772/amid-data-controversy-nsa-builds-its-biggest-data-farm.

[65] Wendy Leung, "Ottawa Airport to Start Recording Your Private Conversations," *Globe and Mail* (June 18, 2012); Ray Locker, "Intelligency Agency Seeks Facial Recognition Upgrade," *USA Today* (November 12, 2013).

[66] Jonathan Finn, *Capturing the Criminal Image: From Mug Shot to Surveillance Society* (Minnesota: University of Minnesota Press, 2009), 94.

our cities.[67] I could continue, but I suspect those committed to believing our private realm is as strong as ever will not be swayed by any amount of evidence to the contrary.

Perhaps we can justify some such developments for the benefits they might bring. It might also be that individuals do not experience them as privacy violations. That, however, is not my point. My concern is with how such initiatives reduce the reality of privacy, irrespective of whether we can rationalize or tolerate unique surveillance measures.

Others will see my comments as too sweeping, and accuse me of not accentuating privacy's nuances and countervailing tendencies. In fact, we urgently need both approaches – those focusing on the details, as well as those that look to the bigger picture. Details, however, appear disjointed and ultimately random without trying to discern broader trends. Focusing on the forest risks missing some trees, but attending only to the trees overlooks our political ecology. And again, I recognize privacy has won important victories, victories I applaud and do not want to see reversed. Nonetheless, the general trend has undeniably been in the direction of greater surveillance and less privacy.

I am also likely to be criticized for being an economic reductionist because I accentuate the power of corporations to alter existing privacy structures to ensure access to our

---

[67] Medea Benjamin, *Drone Warfare: Killing by Remote Control* (New York: Verso, 2013); Patrick White, "Unmanned Drone Prowls Over the Lonely Prairie," *Globe and Mail* (February 18, 2009).

personal data. In fact, I am attuned to the operation of chance and contingency, and recognize how social developments are determined by multiple causal factors. Human agency can undeniably check menacing developments. If change was not possible I would not bother to write about such issues. That said, it is foolhardy to ignore the demonstrated ability of corporate actors to shape laws and regulatory structures to advance their ambitions. If I have placed too much weight on how corporations can or will transform the privacy infrastructure – which I doubt – then it is a necessary corrective to privacy analysts' general neglect of the powers of informational capitalism.

Still others will say I am being alarmist. My emphasis on the threat of authoritarian forms of rule inherent in populations open to detailed institutional scrutiny will be portrayed as overblown and overdramatic, suggesting I veer towards the lunatic fringe of unhinged conspiracy theorists.[68] But one does not have to believe secret forces are operating behind the scenes to recognize that our declining private realm presents alarming dangers. Someone as conservative and deeply embedded in the security establishment as William Binney – a former NSA senior executive – says the security surveillance infrastructure he helped build now puts us on the verge of "turnkey totalitarianism."[69]

---

[68] Mark Fenster, *Conspiracy Theories: Secrecy and Power in American Culture* (Minnesota: University of Minnesota Press, 2008).

[69] James Bamford, "The NSA Is Building the Country's Biggest Spy Centre (Watch What You Say)", *Wired* (March 15, 2012).

The contemporary expansion of surveillance, where monitoring becomes an ever-more routine part of our lives, represents a tremendous shift in the balance of power between citizens and organizations. Perhaps the greatest danger of this situation is how our existing surveillance practices can be turned to oppressive uses. From this point forward our expanding surveillance infrastructure stands as a resource to be inherited by future generations of politicians, corporate actors, or even messianic leaders. Given sufficient political will, this surveillance infrastructure can be re-purposed to monitor – in unparalleled detail – people who some might see as undesirable due to their political opinions, religion, skin color, gender, birthplace, physical abilities, medical history, or any number of an almost limitless list of factors used to pit people against one another.

The twentieth century provides notorious examples of such repressive uses of surveillance. Crucially, those tyrannical states exercised fine-grained political control by relying on surveillance infrastructures that today seem laughably rudimentary, composed as they were of paper files, index cards, and elementary telephone tapping.[70]

It is no more alarmist to acknowledge such risks are germane to our own societies than it is to recognize the future will see wars, terrorist attacks, or environmental disasters –

[70] Anna Funder, *Stasiland: True Stories from Behind the Berln Wall* (London: Granta, 2003); John C. Schmeidel, *Stasi* (London: Routledge, 2008).

events that could themselves prompt surveillance structures to be re-calibrated towards more coercive ends. Those who think this massive surveillance infrastructure will not, in the fullness of time, be turned to repressive purposes are either innocent as to the realities of power, or whistling past a graveyard.

But one does not have to dwell on the most extreme possibilities to be unnerved by how enhanced surveillance capabilities invest tremendous powers in organizations. Surveillance capacity gives organizations unprecedented abilities to manipulate human behaviors, desires, and sub-jectivities towards organizational ends – ends that are too often focused on profit, personal aggrandizement, and insti-tutional self-interest rather than human betterment.

One final criticism of my position will undoubtedly be that I do not offer an alternative. This is admittedly true. For years this lack of an alternative postponed my turning my attention to this topic. But we do not necessarily expect the scientists, physicians, or engineers who identify a prob-lem to provide a solution. For communities of physicians or researchers to wholeheartedly commit to searching for new treatments someone must first accentuate how existing rem-edies do not work. At a minimum I see my contribution in this light. I hope to disturb the otherwise unflagging faith among legislators that introducing new privacy laws amounts to an effective way to halt the expansion of surveillance.

The extent to which readers identify with my character-ization of the privacy situation may come down to a question of what fears animate our politics, and our perception of what current trends prefigure. In time I expect we will profoundly regret forging a world where a hybrid of governmental and private agencies have unprecedented access to the minutiae of our physical movements, relationships, communications, tastes, reading habits, religious beliefs, ethnicity, consumption patterns, sexual orientation, medical history, finances, addictions, and so on. When we look back on how this happened one factor that will stand out will be the inability of the privacy establishment to meaningfully check the expansion of surveillance.

Or perhaps my despondency should be laid at my own feet, and at the feet of those who shared my early faith that privacy laws and data protection regimes would provide a more effective defense against the spread of surveillance. For, you see, in 1985 I was one of those people who believed in the anti-surveillance possibilities of privacy laws.

Afterword

Responding to a World Without Privacy: On the Potential Merits of a Comparative Law Perspective

Ronald J. Krotoszynski, Jr.

The contributions to this book present a rich mosaic on a critically important topic: namely, how best to respond to the growing and ever-present threats to privacy. The authors provide an engaging and provocative exploration of highly salient themes related to the question of the status of privacy in contemporary society – and how and whether we could improve our efforts to advance privacy interests.

My purpose in this concluding chapter is to find a common theme or idea that helps to unite each of the distinguished authors' contributions and that relates these contributions to each other. The most obvious point of tangency is that they all demonstrate the centrality and importance of privacy as a legal and cultural construct; those who claim privacy is dead need only peruse these chapters to see that the concept retains tremendous salience in legal, policy, and cultural terms. A second point on which the contributors appear to agree is that modern technology and the advent of metadata present a real and growing threat to the concept of privacy as non-disclosure. A third point of common concern relates to how each of the authors finds it necessary to engage the public–private distinction.[1] This is not surprising; threats to privacy arise not only from the actions of the state, but also through the actions of private companies that collect, store, and exploit personal data. Privacy claims certainly arise against the government, but they also arise against private actors with great frequency as well.[2]

Professor Kevin Haggerty argues that the massive data gathering and sorting capacities – held in both government

---

[1] Morton J. Horwitz, "The History of the Public/Private Distinction," *University of Pennsylvania Law Review* 130 (1982), 1423.

[2] David P. Currie, "Positive and Negative Constitutional Rights," *University of Chicago Law Review* 53 (1986), 861, 883–886 notes that although constitutional rights in the United States generally run only against the state, in many European systems constitutional rights not only bind the state itself but also create positive state duties to secure constitutional values more comprehensively within the general community through positive regulations of private behavior; Ronald J. Krotoszynski, Jr., "Back to the Briarpatch: An Argument in Favor of Constitutional Meta-Analysis in State Action Determinations," *Michigan Law Review* 94 (1995), 302 discusses and critiques the state action doctrine's relevance to limiting the scope and effects of constitutional rights.

and private hands – make protecting against both government and non-government privacy depredations a difficult, if not impossible task.[3] He asks whether "the laws designed to protect privacy, when looked at as a whole, offer realistic hope of insulating us from the powerful forces coalescing to reduce the reality of privacy."[4] Haggerty laments that "[o]ver the course of many decades surveillance has expanded and intensified almost everywhere, becoming a dominant organizing practice."[5]

Several other contributions actively engage the problem of private power with respect to privacy. Professor Rebecca Tushnet, for example, focuses her contribution on the problem of permitting private parties to banish anonymous or pseudonymous speech from highly visible – and successful – social media platforms.[6] She criticizes Google for prohibiting the use of anonymous or pseudonymous posts on Google+ and objects to Google CEO Eric Schmidt's casual dismissal of objections to these practices because, as he puts it, people who seek to post content on Google+ without attribution "just shouldn't use it."[7] Thus, private power, no less than public power, sets the metes and bounds of privacy as non-disclosure.

---

[3] Kevin D. Haggerty, "What's Wrong With Privacy Protections? Provocations from a Fifth Columnist," in *A World Without Privacy*, ed. Austin D. Sarat (Cambridge: Cambridge University Press, 2015).

[4] *Ibid.*, 194.

[5] *Ibid.*, 201.

[6] Rebecca Tushnet, "The Yes Men and The Women Men Don't See," in *A World Without Privacy*, ed. Austin D. Sarat (Cambridge: Cambridge University Press, 2015).

[7] *Ibid.*, 109.

The most obvious potential means of checking private power to promote privacy interests would involve the use of governmental power to regulate corporate exploitation of individuals' private information and data. However, for some of the reasons set forth quite ably by Professor Haggerty, the state itself also constitutes a significant part of the problem. Thus, effectively safeguarding privacy presents a multivariate and complex task.

Given that many of the current threats to privacy simply do not respect national borders, we should, as Justice Elena Kagan has posited, seek good ideas wherever we can find them.[8] In other words, rather than merely guessing about the potential efficacy of responses to the growing threats to privacy, it would make more sense to consider whether particular regulatory approaches have proven successful – or unsuccessful – in other polities that share a commitment to safeguarding the reasonable privacy expectations of the citizenry. The balance of this afterword considers why and how a comparative legal perspective might help to improve our

[8] At her confirmation hearings, Justice Elena Kagan explained that she did not think it appropriate for the Supreme Court to afford formal precedential value to foreign legal decisions. However, Justice Kagan added that she was very much "in favor of good ideas coming from wherever you can get them" and suggested that "there are a number of circumstances" in which considering foreign law as persuasive authority could be both helpful and appropriate. Confirmation Hearing on The Nomination of Elena Kagan to be an Associate Justice of the Supreme Court of the United States: Hearing Before the Sen. Comm. on the Judiciary, 111th Cong. 127 (2010).

approach to dealing with the growing reality of a world without privacy.

I. The case for a comparative analysis of privacy

All of the contributions to this volume reflect assumptions and understandings that are drawn largely from local, or domestic, privacy regimes; yet, these local understandings and balances will not necessarily hold true across national boundaries and cultures. Simply put, the protection of privacy in other democratic nations reflects a core of common concerns, but also different legal, social, and moral understandings of privacy rights. The chapters individually and collectively suggest the potential utility of comparative legal analysis for reconsidering the problem of reduced privacy in our digital world – as well as some possible means of arresting the trend toward diminished privacy against both the government and corporate entities such as Microsoft, Google, and Facebook. In fact, several of the authors directly use comparative legal perspectives to advance their arguments.

Both Lisa Austin[9] and Kevin Haggerty[10] draw on comparative law to challenge existing baselines in the United

---

[9] Lisa Austin, "Enough About Me: Why Privacy Is About Consent, Not Power," in *A World Without Privacy*, ed. Austin D. Sarat (Cambridge: Cambridge University Press, 2015).

[10] Haggerty, "What's Wrong with Privacy Protections," 205–209, 220–221.

States. Moreover, the themes and issues that Professor Richards (privacy myths)[11] and Professor Tushnet (anonymous speech and privacy)[12] engage and explore could benefit from comparative legal analysis. To be clear, I do not claim that privacy must necessarily be considered through a comparative law lens – purely domestic treatment of privacy regulation can and does work quite well. And, in many respects, consideration of privacy through a purely domestic lens makes a great deal of sense. Privacy on the ground is, after all, largely a function of local law.

The relevant question is not whether a comparative law perspective is essential, but rather whether it might be useful. I do not suggest that we should collectively strive toward the creation of some sort of global law of privacy; nor would I suggest some kind of Platonic Idea of privacy floats lazily above our heads, just waiting to be discovered and deployed for the benefit of each and every one of us. Nor would I posit that foreign privacy law is plainly superior to existing baselines in the United States or Canada.

My point is considerably more limited: I only suggest that knowledge and consideration of foreign privacy regimes could assist us in assessing the virtues and shortcomings of our contemporary domestic arrangements. Armed with better knowledge of potential alternative solutions to solving the

---

[11] Neil M. Richards, "Four Privacy Myths," in *A World Without Privacy*, ed. Austin D. Sarat (Cambridge: Cambridge University Press, 2015).

[12] Tushnet, "The Yes Men ..."

problem of effectively safeguarding privacy interests we might, or might not, elect to revisit our existing domestic approach. However, even if we elect not to revise our domestic regulation of privacy, our law of privacy would surely be the better for undertaking the exercise.

Allow me to begin with a single example: the use of the concept of a "reasonable expectation of privacy" as a test for ascertaining whether an individual has a viable constitutional privacy claim. Professor Haggerty worries that use of "a reasonable expectation of privacy" metric to delimit privacy interests will routinely lead to the underprotection of privacy in the era of big data because "those expectations change in relation to personal experiences."[13] He adds that "[a]s surveillance becomes an ever-more routine aspect of our lives the public's privacy expectations appear to be declining, and the courts will undoubtedly appeal to this tendency to justify further limitations on privacy."[14]

Perhaps this is so, but perhaps it is not. In fact, I am not at all sure that the precise legal framework used to protect privacy interests matters more than the substantive outcomes in concrete cases. To state the matter simply, language, even legal terms of art, can be misleading. For example, a legal standard resting on a person's "reasonable expectation of privacy" need not be a descriptive, or

[13] Haggerty, "What's Wrong with Privacy Protections," 205.
[14] Ibid.

empirical, concept; instead, it could easily be normative or aspirational in both its character and operation.

As it happens, the Supreme Court of Canada has squarely held that Section 8 of the Canadian Charter of Rights and Freedoms, which prohibits unreasonable searches and seizures,[15] only protects a "reasonable expectation of privacy." However, the Supreme Court of Canada has taken great care to emphasize that this is *not* an empirical standard, but rather a *normative* standard. In *R. v. Tessling*, Justice Binnie explains that:

> In an age of expanding means for snooping readily available on the retail market, ordinary people may come to fear (with or without justification) that their telephones are wiretapped or their private correspondence is being read ... Suggestions that a diminished *subjective* expectation of privacy should automatically result in a lowering of constitutional protection should therefore be opposed. It is one thing to say that a person who puts out the garbage has no reasonable expectation of privacy in it. It is quite another to say that someone who fears their telephone is bugged no longer has a *subjective* expectation of privacy and thereby forfeits the protection of s. 8. Expectation of privacy is a normative rather than a descriptive standard.[16]

---

[15] Constitution Act, 1982, ch. 11, Schedule B, Part 1, Canadian Charter of Rights and Freedoms, 8; Everyone has the right to be secure against unreasonable search or seizure [hereinafter "Canadian Charter"].

[16] *R. v. Tessling*, [2004] 3 S.C.R. 432, 452, para. 42 (Can.).; see also *R. v Plant*, [1993] 3 S.C.R. 281, 293 (Can.) (holding that a person's

Accordingly, as the Court explained in *Patrick*, even if government "increases its snooping on the lives of its citizens, and thereby makes them suspicious and reduces their expectations of privacy,"[17] such action "will not thereby succeed in unilaterally reducing their constitutional entitlement to privacy protection."[18]

Thus, the assumption that a "reasonable expectation of privacy" metric will necessarily permit the creeping advance of technology to render the concept of privacy archaic does not necessarily hold true. If defined in purposive and normative terms, rather than by reference to what people actually expect of the government or their internet service provider, it could conceivably convey significant protection to personal privacy interests.

The legal standard used to define the scope of privacy rights provides only a single example of how a comparative law perspective could enhance our understanding of privacy. Certainly, other examples exist. Our understanding of privacy could be enriched and expanded were we to consider how other democratic polities have drawn the metes and bounds of individual autonomy, the right of non-disclosure, and the ability to control the dissemination of information that relates to our identities.

> reasonable expectation of privacy should be defined in light of larger societal values, including "the underlying values of dignity, integrity and autonomy" and that s. 8 analysis must involve a careful "balancing of the societal interests in protecting individual dignity, integrity and autonomy with effective law enforcement").

[17] *R. v. Patrick*, [2009] 1 S.C.R. 579, 591, para. 14 (Can.).
[18] *Ibid.*

Finally, it also bears noting that the precise nomenclature used to safeguard privacy rights appears to matter less than the scope and substance of the substantive interests protected. This is a lesson that comparative law can teach. For example, Germany's Basic Law does not contain a privacy provision of any kind; it speaks instead to "human dignity,"[19] "free development of the personality,"[20] and "personal honor."[21] Yet, despite the absence of an express right of privacy, interests sounding in "privacy" in US law and culture are, generally speaking, more reliably and more robustly protected in Germany than in the United States.

In fact, the cultural salience of privacy is undoubtedly a better marker for the protection of privacy interests than the precise nomenclature deployed in its service. A society that expects privacy will enjoy more of it than one that does not; this is not a function of "reasonable expectations" but rather simply a fact of political economy; both politicians and judges will respect an expectation more reliably and more completely

---

[19] Grundgesetz Für die Bundesrepublik Deutschland [Grundgesetz] [GG] [Basic Law], May 23, 1949, BGBl. I, Art. 1 (Ger.) ("Human dignity shall be inviolable. To respect and protect it shall be the duty of all state authority").

[20] *Ibid.*, Art. 2 ("Every person shall have the right to free development of his personality insofar as he does not violate the rights of others or offend against the constitutional order or the moral law.").

[21] *Ibid.*, Art. 5(2) (providing that protection of freedom of expression under Article 5(1) does not require invalidation of laws adopted in order to safeguard "the right to personal honor.").

when a right enjoys broad social and cultural salience within a society.

Thus, in the United States, freedom of speech enjoys a more reliable, and broader, scope of protection because it possesses more social and cultural relevance than, say, privacy – legal protection is more often than not a function of social and cultural expectations. European privacy law is more rigorous not because European politicians are more virtuous, but rather because privacy enjoys broader and deeper social and cultural relevance there. As Professor Whitman observes, "[d]ifferences in cultural tradition, in short, have made for palpable differences in law."[22] Moreover, "[t]he differences [between the United States and Europe] are most striking, and most categorical, where the values of free speech are involved."[23]

II. The problem of technology, the creeping loss of privacy, and the critical importance of cultural norms in shaping privacy law

A common lament is that, in light of data gathering capacities held in both governmental and private hands, the concept of privacy has fallen into a state of desuetude. A comparative law perspective would help to give the lie to the notion that

[22] James Q. Whitman, "The Two Western Cultures of Privacy: Dignity Versus Liberty," *Yale Law Journal* 113 (2004), 1151, 1196.
[23] *Ibid.*

technology, of necessity, must redefine or reshape our existing social norms and expectations. Indeed, the core premise that we are simply prisoners of technology rings false – at least when viewed from a comparative law perspective.

For example, in many European jurisdictions, including France and Germany, employers may not routinely engage in surveillance of their employees – even for legitimate purposes such as avoiding shirking and ensuring adequate productivity.[24] As Whitman observes, "[c]ontinental law has made considerable efforts to guarantee the privacy of workers in the workplace, at least within the limits of the possible."[25] Privacy protections in the workplace extend to "workers' private documents, guarantees against video surveillance, and rights to use telephones for personal calls – all in the name of maintaining a 'personal sphere.'"[26] Thus, the cultural baseline in countries such as France and Germany appears to be sufficiently robust to withstand the oncoming tide of technology to facilitate snooping – at least in the workplace context. Simply put, in France and Germany, electronic snooping by employers is illegal and this proscription is vigorously enforced.[27]

My point is that culture informs law and that cultural expectations can play an important role in determining the

---

[24] See Whitman, "Two Western Cultures," 1156, 1194–1196.

[25] *Ibid.*, 1194.

[26] *Ibid.*, 1194–1195.

[27] *Ibid.*, 1194. As Whitman explains, "[t]his is law that protects employees against being addressed disrespectfully, shunned, or even assigned humiliating tasks like xeroxing." *Ibid.*, 1165.

effective protection of privacy on the ground. I do not suggest that law is irrelevant, but in the area of privacy, I tend to think that law generally tracks culture. For example, imagine the legal response in the United States if Walmart were to install cameras in its employee bathrooms – to monitor employees for bad behavior and to prevent shirking. Does anyone think that our legal system, at least in 2014, would fail to respond effectively to such a development?[28] This example helps to demonstrate concretely how culture prefixes the scope of legal protection of privacy; in France, expectations of privacy are broader than in the United States, but even in the United States we can and do protect privacy in the workplace.

Other examples of how culture informs law exist and could be quite relevant to rethinking the "inevitable" effects of new technology on the scope of privacy in the United States. For example, the Supreme Court of Canada has decoupled privacy protection from the ownership of property, such that a government employee or a student could claim a

---

[28] Professor Haggerty has called my attention to the utter lack of employee privacy that prevailed during the Industrial Revolution and well into the twentieth century; I do not doubt that his historical point is entirely accurate. However, many practices commonplace in the Gilded Age would not be tolerated in 2014 including, for example, the routine use of child labor. The question is not whether any society could be imagined that failed to protect a particular kind of privacy interest; instead, the question is whether contemporary society would countenance a particular kind of privacy loss without objection or push back.

constitutional privacy interest in data contained on a computer owned and maintained by the government (in the form of an employer or a school).[29] By way of contrast, the US approach, reflected in Justice Scalia's majority opinion in *United States v. Jones*,[30] reflects a tethering of privacy to property. In *Jones*, Justice Scalia explains that "our Fourth Amendment jurisprudence was tied to common-law trespass, at least until the latter half of the 20th century,"[31] and observes that "for most of our history the Fourth Amendment was understood to embody a particular concern for government trespass upon the areas … it enumerates."[32]

A property-based approach to securing privacy rights presents one model; a consent-based approach presents another. Both models possess advantages and shortcomings. A comparative legal analysis might help us to choose between them – as well as other possible framing devices for the protection of privacy interests.

With respect to a consent-based approach to securing privacy, Professor Austin observes that "[t]hese structural defects [in consent-based privacy regimes] bring us full circle back to the problem to which a consent-based model of privacy looked so promising as a solution."[33] The problem is that

---

[29] See *R. v. Cole*, [2012] 3 S.C.R. 34, 45, para. 28 (Can.).

[30] 132 S. Ct. 945 (2012).

[31] *Ibid.*, 949.

[32] *Ibid.*, 950.

[33] Austin, "Enough About Me," 144.

"consent proves rather anemic, in need of revitalizing through other ... ideas of privacy."[34]

As an alternative, Austin suggests that a more open-ended rule, drawing on rule-of-law values related to the common law's privileging of property, might have more potential for enhancing individual power, and hence control, over their personal data. Austin posits that:

> The consent model is frequently described either in terms of property or in terms of strengthening it through making it more like property. In this spirit, but departing from the standard analyses along these lines, I argue that there are two significant lessons that privacy law can take from our ideas of trespass. First, the trespass roots of constitutional guarantees against unreasonable search and seizure point us to the importance of basic rule-of-law values that have long underpinned the constitutional right to privacy. We need much more explicit attention to these values, along with an understanding of the role that private sector organizations, and citizens more generally, play in both upholding them and being constrained by them. I call this the "power-over" analysis.[35]

On the other hand, however, linking privacy to more abstract rule-of-law notions could easily diminish the scope of privacy interests in many important contexts where the government can claim a managerial or proprietary right to snoop.[36]

---

[34] *Ibid.*

[35] *Ibid.*, 160.

[36] See Robert Post, "Subsidized Speech," *Yale Law Journal* 106 (1996): 151, 164–167, 184–190, 194–195.

Austin is surely right to focus on effective control and empowerment of the individual citizen, but the best means to securing more effective control appear uncertain to me.

To the extent that consent is not really meaningful or voluntary, it does little (if anything) to address the core problem of private companies collecting and redistributing personal information. If "consent" reduces to the equivalent of a shrink wrap contract,[37] it does not bespeak agreement in any ordinary sense of the word.

Although I cannot offer any easy or elegant solutions to the problem, perhaps the same technology that gives rise to new privacy challenges can be redeployed in the service of privacy. Moreover, the problem of collective action also requires attention – just as laws protecting collective bargaining were essential to leveling the playing field between labor and management,[38] it might well be that similar

---

[37] See Florencia Marotta-Wurgler, "Will Increased Disclosure Help? Evaluating the Recommendations of the ALI's 'Principles of the Law of Software Contracts,'" *University of Chicago Law Review* 78 (2011), 165, which questions whether proposed ALI reforms to shrink-wrap contract terms for software licenses go far enough in protecting consumers from arbitrary and unfair contract terms; Florencia Marotta-Wurgler, "What's in a Standard Form Contract? An Empirical Analysis of Software Licensing Agreements," *Journal of Empirical Legal Studies* 4 (2007), 677, which notes that most standard terms on shrink-wrap software licensing agreements reflect a strong bias toward software companies and that consumers lack much, if not all, bargaining power to obtain more fair terms.

[38] See The National Labor Relations Act, ch. 372, 49 Stat. 449 (1935) (codified as amended 29 U.S.C. §§ 151–169 (2012)).

government interventions in favor of equalizing the bargaining power between computer users and entities that collect personal data would constitute a logical response. In short, "power-over," to use Austin's turn of phrase, might well require collective bargaining power rather than efforts to increase individual agency. And, once again, a comparative legal perspective would be quite useful in attempting to work out effective solutions to these thorny problems.

III. Reconsidering privacy and the role of the state in the era of "big data"

Without doubt, many of the most pressing threats to privacy involve government efforts to amass vast quantities of information about citizens and businesses alike (the problem of "big data"). As Professor Haggerty suggests, the implications of this vast information dragnet for the project of democratic self-government are deeply troubling.[39]

At the same time, however, the state need not be the enemy of privacy – it could be the only potential means of checking vast agglomerations of private power that can be deployed to invade privacy. In fact, given the problems of collective action, individual consumers have little effective power against monopoly or oligopoly internet service providers; so too, an individual lacks any meaningful bargaining power against a Microsoft, a Google, or a Facebook. The state presents the only potential

---

[39] Haggerty, "What's Wrong With Privacy Protections," 200–201, 212–223.

check on the unregulated use of private corporate power to compromise privacy. Moreover, when your personality is being digitized and commoditized, the better to manipulate your electoral and market choices, the state actor status of the entity undertaking the snooping matters less – or should matter less – than the fact of the snooping itself.

Owen Fiss has written cogently about the need to consider state interventions in speech markets with some care – rather than reflexive skepticism.[40] This is so because only the state possesses the ability to check potential dysfunctions that result from the use of private power to distort speech markets. As Fiss observes, "[i]n another world things might be different, but in this one, we will need the state."[41] Thus, "[j]ust as it is no longer possible to assume that the private sector is all freedom, we can no longer assume that the state is all censorship."[42] These observations plainly apply with full force to state interventions in the private market to protect personal privacy.

The contributors clearly understand the Janus-like nature of the state with respect to privacy: on the one hand,

---

[40] See Owen M. Fiss, "Why the State?," *Harvard Law Review* 100 (1987), 781, 787–791; Owen M. Fiss, "Free Speech and Social Structure," *Iowa Law Review* 71 (1986), 1405, 1412–1416; Owen M. Fiss, "Silence on the Street Corner," *Suffolk University Law Review* 26 (1992), 1–3. Fiss posits that "[t]he state should be allowed to intervene, and sometimes even required to do so ... to correct for the market." Fiss, "Why the State," 791.

[41] Fiss, "Why the State," 794.

[42] Fiss, "Free Speech and Social Structure," 1415.

government regulation in places such as Canada, as Professor Austin observes, has been deployed successfully to safeguard consumer privacy against private and public depredations.[43] In other cases, however, the absence of regulation has left privacy regulation to the not-so-tender mercies of the market.

We also should be careful not to become enthralled with privacy clichés – that is to say, we should not rely on easy over-generalizations about privacy as an excuse for failing to interrogate existing privacy narratives effectively or carefully. Professor Richards is quite correct to raise, and then debunk, some commonly accepted "truths" about the nature of privacy and privacy regulation.[44] Privacy is not dead, people continue to expect privacy, and do so regardless of whether they perceive themselves as having anything to hide, and it's not clear whether stronger privacy protections would enhance, rather than degrade, the myriad goods, services, and opportunities available on the internet or otherwise.[45]

We could also consider whether the state should have the luxury of electing to remain neutral in the face of growing privacy disputes between individuals and private corporations. For example, in the jurisprudence of the European

---

[43] Austin, "Enough About Me," 134–138 (discussing the main Canadian federal privacy law, the Personal Information and Electronic Documents Act, known as PIPEDA, and its reliance on privacy commissioners to help secure privacy in Canada).

[44] See Richards, "Four Privacy Myths," 33–34, 81–82.

[45] *Ibid.*, 35–50.

Court of Human Rights (ECHR), human rights have both positive and negative dimensions – they are "freedoms from" but also affirmative "rights to."[46] Nor are these interests necessarily bounded by "property" as such; in other words, broader protection of privacy could be achieved simply by rethinking the state's duty with respect to the safeguarding of fundamental rights more broadly within society.

To provide a concrete example, Article 8 of the European Convention for the Protection of Human Rights and Fundamental Freedoms (European Convention), which provides that "Everyone has the right to respect for his private and family life, his home and his correspondence,"[47] creates a positive obligation on the part of signatory governments to secure these values comprehensively within the community; fundamental human rights, under this approach, should permeate all aspects of the society – and not just interactions with the state itself. As the ECHR has explained, "[t]hese obligations may involve the adoption of measures designed to secure respect for private life even in the sphere of the relations of individuals between themselves."[48]

---

[46] See, for example, *X and Y v. The Netherlands*, Application No. 8978/80, 8 Eur. H.R. Rep. 235, 239–240 (1985) (decided March 26, 1985).

[47] Convention for the Protection of Human Rights and Fundamental Freedoms, Nov. 4, 1950, 213 U.N.T.S 222, C.E.T.S. 5, Article 8 (1) [hereinafter "European Convention"].

[48] *X and Y v. The Netherlands.*, *supra* note 46, at 239–240, para. 23. To be sure, the primary focus of Article 8 "is essentially that of protecting the individual against arbitrary interference by public authorities." *Ibid.* However, it is a necessary, but not sufficient,

Thus, we should not assume that human rights need only be conceptualized in negative terms; it's perfectly plausible to think of human rights as involving a governmental obligation to secure these values broadly within society as a whole – rather than solely as a mandate against government violations. The concept of positive rights raises interesting possibilities about government's duty to protect citizens from private acts that burden or abridge rights.[49] This approach to enforcing fundamental rights has not gained much ground in the United States,[50] but many state constitutions have privacy guarantees[51] and a state supreme court would be

condition for the state itself to refrain from violating European Convention rights, including the right of privacy set forth in Article 8.

[49] But cf. *DeShaney v. Winnebago Ctny. Dep't of Soc. Servs.*, 489 U.S. 189, 195–196 (1989), holding that state governments lack any general duty of care toward children within their jurisdiction, even if a state agency has actual knowledge that a particular child faces threats to his health and safety.

[50] *Ibid.*, 195, which held that "nothing in the language of the Due Process Clause itself requires the State to protect the life, liberty, and property of its citizens against invasion by private actor."

[51] See Jeffrey M. Shaman, "The Right of Privacy in State Constitutional Law," *Rutgers Law Journal* 37 (2006), 971, 974–976, which discusses state constitutional privacy guarantees; see also Julie E. Flanagan, Note, "Restricting Electronic Monitoring in the Private Workplace," *Duke Law Journal* 43 (1994), 1256, 1265, which notes the existence of state constitutional privacy guarantees and lists illustrative provisions in the footnotes; Kevin P. Kopp, "Electronic Communications in the Workplace: Email Monitoring and the Right of Privacy," *Seton Hall Constitutional Law Journal* 8

entirely free to interpret such a clause to require affirmative state government efforts to secure privacy more broadly within its jurisdiction.[52]

In sum, a particularly relevant baseline question relates to the proper role of the state in securing privacy. On the one hand, state power presents the most significant threat to personal privacy. The recent revelations by Edward Snowden demonstrate quite clearly that government power can be, and will be, used in ways that defeat reasonable expectations of privacy.[53] On the other hand,

(1998), 861, 867, notes that "[u]nlike the Federal Constitution, many state constitutions explicitly guarantee a right of privacy".

[52] In this regard, state constitutions commonly include positive rights, such as clauses that guarantee a right to a free and public education. See William J. Brennan, Jr., "State Constitutions and the Protection of Individual Rights," *Harvard Law Review* 90 (1977), 489; James Gardner, "State Constitutional Rights as Resistance to National Power: Toward a Functional Theory of State Constitutions," *Georgetown Law Journal* 91 (2003), 1003; Helen Hershkoff, "Positive Rights and State Constitutions: The Limits of Federal Rationality Review," *Harvard Law Review* 112 (1999), 1131; Burt Neuborne, "Forword: State Constitutions and the Evolution of Positive Rights," *Rutgers Law Journal* 20 (1989), 881. For a more skeptical view of the potential utility of positive rights in state constitutions to advance fundamental rights, see Jeffrey Omar Usman, "Good Enough for Government Work: The Interpretation of Positive Constitutional Rights in State Constitutions," *Albany Law Review* 73 (1999), 1459.

[53] See Michael Birnbaum & Ellen Nakashima, "U.S. Accused of Eavesdropping on German President," *Washington Post* (October 24, 2013), discussing Edward Snowden's revelations regarding the NSA's PRISM program and their effect in the United States and Europe; Barton Gellman & Laura Poitras, "U.S. Intelligence Mining

however, average citizens lack the ability to negotiate effectively with corporate entities such as Microsoft, Google, and Facebook; only the state has the ability to check successfully the use of private market power to undermine personal privacy. Given this duality, it would be particularly useful to consider under what circumstances government interventions on behalf of privacy have proven successful – and when such interventions have failed. A comparative law perspective could offer a very useful lens for analyzing these important questions.

IV. Anonymous speech as a protected form of privacy

Anonymity and its regulation provide another excellent topic for comparative law study; societies vary in the extent to which they tolerate anonymous or pseudonymous speech. Professor Tushnet argues that anonymity on the internet can have the effect of creating space and distance that empowers persons at the margins of society to participate

Data from Nine U.S. Internet Companies in Broad Secret Program," Washington Post (June 6, 2012), discusses the NSA's massive global spying program on both global rivals and ostensible allies of the United States; Glenn Greenwald & Ewen MacAskill, "NSA Taps in to Internet Giants," *The Guardian* (June 6, 2012) discussing the same issue; see also Barton Gellman, "U.S. Surveillance Architecture Includes Collection of Revealing Internet, Phone Metadata," *Washington Post* (June 15, 2013), discussing the scope of the NSA's PRISM program.

more vigorously in the marketplace of ideas and the project of democratic self-government.[54]

I would cheerfully accede to the suggestion that anonymity, or the use of a pseudonym, can empower persons who lack social, economic, or political power within a particular community – and particularly members of minority groups (however defined). But there's a dark side to anonymous and pseudonymous speech as well: the same anonymity that protects a woman criticizing the failure of the armed forces to deal effectively with sexual assault empowers the government itself to propagandize the population.

Professor Lyrissa Barnett Lidsky has cautioned about the potential distortionary effects of government entities using social media to communicate with citizens.[55] She notes, quite accurately, that "[t]he government has begun to convey its message through emails, websites, Facebook pages, tweets, and text messages."[56] And, in seeking to prod citizens to action, "[g]overnments seek to persuade, manipulate, coerce, nudge, wheedle, and imprecate."[57] Lidsky also acknowledges that "[a] skeptic could argue that social media may make it easier for the government to disseminate propaganda"[58] but suggests that "this argument is

[54] Tushnet, "The Yes Men ...," 88–91, 122–130.
[55] Lyrissa Lidsky, "Public Forum 2.0," *Boston University Law Review* 91 (2011), 1975, 2002–2004.
[56] *Ibid.*, 2003.
[57] *Ibid.*
[58] *Ibid.*, 2007.

misplaced."[59] On the other hand, however, government use of social media can be beneficial and enhance the scope and relevance of public involvement in the process of democratic self-government.[60] Professor Lidsky plainly anticipates that such government interventions in the social media marketplace will be transparent – and not anonymous or otherwise hidden – whether on a voluntary basis or through the intermediation of the press.[61]

On a decidedly less optimistic note, however, Professor Gia Lee has characterized the government's use of anonymous or pseudonymous speech to attempt to hide its authorship of comments from the citizenry as clearly and deeply problematic.[62] Lee argues that "applied in the government speech context, the political accountability principle calls for governments to speak 'in full view of the public'" rather than through the use of pseudonymous sock puppets.[63] Simply put, "governments ought not to have the same freedom to speak as private parties."[64]

---

[59] Ibid.

[60] See ibid., 2004–2008, discussing the potential benefits associated with greater use of social media by government entities.

[61] See ibid., 2002–2010.

[62] Gia B. Lee, "Persuasion, Transparency, and Government Speech," Hastings Law Journal 56 (2005), 983, 1009–1026; see also Lyrissa Barnett Lidsky, "Silencing John Doe: Defamation & Discourse in Cyberspace," Duke Law Journal 49 (2000), 855, 896–897; Helen Norton & Danielle Keats Citron, "Government Speech 2.0," Denver University Law Review 87 (2010), 899, 936–939.

[63] Lee, "Persuasion, Transparency," 1018.

[64] Ibid.

To provide a concrete example, members of Wisconsin Governor Scott Walker's staff admitted spending paid time posting mis-attributed pro-Walker comments on social media outlets.[65] Similarly, the TSA has been accused of censoring social media and also posing supposedly "private party" comments on social media outlets that frequent travelers use to discuss complaints about TSA policies, procedures, and personnel.[66]

Anonymous speech by the government itself plainly has a distortionary effect on the marketplace of ideas; it impedes, rather than enhances, the ongoing process of democratic deliberation. As Professors Helen Norton and Danielle Citron have observed, "[g]overnment's use of such [anonymous and pseudonymous communications] technologies is troubling if government officials participate without identifying themselves: unidentified authors prevent readers from using a message's governmental source as a cue to its credibility."[67] They argue that "[t]he sock puppetry concern provides further justification for insisting that government

---

[65] Jason Stein, Patrick Marley, & Daniel Bice, "Walker Urged Staff, Aides, to Promote Him Online," *Journal-Sentinel* (Milwaukee, WI) (February 23, 2014)

[66] See http://www.flyertalk.com/forum/practical-travel-safety-issues/ 1172468-bb-rushes-cover-his-employers-back.html (last accessed on March 25, 2014). Complaints include active censoring of comments posted to the TSA's website and the alleged practice of TSA employees posting pro-TSA comments on various social media outlets without identifying themselves as TSA employees.

[67] Norton & Citron, "Government Speech 2.0," 936.

clearly identify itself as a message's source if it wishes to claim the government speech defense."[68]

Corporations and wealthy individuals, such as the Koch brothers, also use anonymous and pseudonymous speech to hide their identities when participating in public debates on the internet. Comments from Lockheed Martin on the necessity of missile defense systems plainly read differently when attributed to an individual citizen.[69] One's trust in government might well prefigure the willingness of the citizenry to permit government regulation of anonymous speech; if one distrusts government, one might well resist regulations aimed at forcing private parties, including corporate speakers, to disclose their identities (or refrain from speaking on the internet). In general, US citizens radically distrust government and therefore tend to view all speech regulations

---

[68] *Ibid.*, 938.

[69] But cf. Lyrissa Barnett Lidsky & Thomas F. Cotter, "Authorship, Audiences, and Anonymous Speech," *Notre Dame Law Review* 82 (2007), 1537, 1548–1556, 1568–1570, 1581–1586, arguing that anonymous and pseudonymous speech has significant social value and should, accordingly, enjoy robust First Amendment protection. In fairness to Lidsky and Cotter, they do stipulate that "the State should have authority to compel speakers to disclose their identities to their audiences when the speakers' autonomy interests are particularly low and the potential for abuse particularly high." *Ibid.*, 1592. On the other hand, however, Lidsky and Cotter also argue that involuntary disclosure of a speaker's identity "cannot be justified absent a compelling need for author identity, at least in the realm of core speech." *Ibid.*, 1602–1603.

with deep misgivings.[70] As I have observed previously, "[t]o a remarkable degree, US citizens mistrust government and seek to minimize its ability to impact their daily lives."[71]

In Europe or Canada, however, the notion that government speech regulations are invariably the product of nefarious schemes or other forms of bad faith simply do not arise as readily, or persist over time as frequently;[72] in such places, regulations of anonymous or pseudonymous speech would be seen as enhancing, rather than degrading, the marketplace of ideas, particularly if such regulations have the effect of equalizing speakers who possess different levels of wealth.[73] In fact, flat bans on privately sponsored

[70] See Ronald J. Krotoszynski, Jr., "The Shot (Not) Heard 'Round the World: Reconsidering the Perplexing U.S. Preoccupation with the Separation of Legislative and Executive Powers," *Boston College Law Review* 51 (2010), 1, 28–34.

[71] *Ibid.*, 30.

[72] See *ibid.*, observing that citizens in places like Canada, France, and Germany "do not view government with the same level of skepticism, if not outright hostility, that US citizens often manifest toward their own governing institutions".

[73] See Ronald J. Krotoszynski, Jr., "Questioning the Value of Dissent and Free Speech More Generally: American Skepticism of Government and the Protection of Low-Value Speech" in *Dissenting Voices in American Society: The Role of Judges, Lawyers, and Citizens*, ed. Austin D. Sarat (Cambridge: Cambridge University Press, 2012), noting that in Canada and most European nations, constitutional courts will generally sustain government regulations of political speech designed to promote equality against free speech and free press objections; see also Krotoszynski, "Shot (Not) Heard," 33, posting that "in a nation sharing a common ethnic, religious, and cultural heritage, trust in government might well come more naturally, and be

issue advertising exist in some places, such as the United Kingdom, as part of regulatory regimes aimed at avoiding the distortion of the political process by those who possess vast private wealth.[74]

I fear that a world without rules with respect to anonymous speech might well do as much to undermine authentic voices as to empower them – given the differentials in wealth, access, and time between the government and corporations, on the one hand, and private individuals, on the other. The presence of anonymous or pseudonymous speech by institutional speakers – whether government agencies or corporations – risks engendering a kind of skepticism toward all such speech on the internet.

Moreover, whether the government itself or publicly traded corporations should have the same right to use anonymous speech or adopt pseudonyms is obviously open to question. As a matter of legal doctrine, however, I suspect that the current Supreme Court would be likely to extend the logic of *Johanns v. Livestock Marketing Ass'n*[75] and *Citizens*

---

held more readily, than in a nation built of immigrants that still features significant divisions based on race, ethnicity, region, urbanization, and culture."

[74] *Animal Defenders Int'l v. United Kingdom*, Application No. 48876/ 08 (decided Apr. 22, 2013) (ECHR) upholding, against an Article 10 objection, the U.K.'s statutory ban on the broadcast of all paid political advertising, other than by recognized political parties, on British television and radio stations, available at http://hudoc. echr.coe.int/sites/fra/pages/search.aspx?i=001–119244#{%22itemid %22:[%22001–119244%22]} (last accessed March 27, 2014).

[75] 544 U.S. 550 (2005).

United v. FEC[76] to cover government and corporate speech of this sort.

If we must choose between a world in which anonymous speech is universally permitted to all would-be speakers, including the government and corporations, or denied to all speakers, including the government and corporations, I'm not at all sure that permitting all speakers to disclaim ownership of their speech would actually do more social good than harm. The easy, and obvious, answer might be to deny government and for-profit corporations the right to speak anonymously – after all, what claim does the government or a publicly traded corporation have to privacy or the need to speak without having comments attributed?[77]

On the other hand, however, the Supreme Court's consistent view that corporate speakers are entitled to no less constitutional protection than real persons should give one pause about the viability of such a distinction under the First Amendment.[78] And the value of information to the recipient, the court held in the *Citizens United* case, is not a function of its source.[79] If there are political benefits to mis-attributing

---

[76] 558 U.S. 310 (2010).

[77] Norton & Citron, "Government Speech 2.0," 933–939, noting the potential dangers associated with mis-attributed government speech.

[78] See Citizens United, 558 U.S. at 341, "The First Amendment protects speech and speaker, and the ideas that flow from each."

[79] *Ibid.*, 340–341, "By taking the right to speak from some and giving it to others, the Government deprives the disadvantaged person or class of the right to use speech to strive to establish worth, standing, and

speech by the powerful and the connected, we should confidently predict that they will use this modality of speech to their full advantage; the system certainly protects persons "marginalized by systems of power,"[80] but it also protects the Koch brothers, General Electric, and the TSA.

The risk of undue corporate power distorting the political process has relevance in another general area of democratic self-government. The use of the citizens initiative provides a cautionary, and potentially instructive, example of how a device intended to empower persons who enjoy marginal political power can be redirected and deployed as a means of enhancing the power of the "haves" – the cost and difficulty of securing the signatures necessary for a ballot initiative make it far more likely that Costco or the NRA will successfully deploy the machinery of the citizens initiative than a small, but determined, group of grass-roots activists who passionately believe that "there ought to be a law."[81]

It is quite easy to romanticize the web as a place that facilitates personal freedom, expression, and self-actualization; certainly, the web advances these values. The internet is

respect for the speaker's voice. The Government may not by these means deprive the public of the right and privilege to determine for itself what speech and speakers are worthy of consideration."

[80] Tushnet, "The Yes Men ...," 111–112 (internal quotation omitted).

[81] See Ronald J. Krotoszynski, Jr., *Reclaiming the Petition Clause: Seditious Libel, "Offensive" Protest, and the Right to Petition the Government for a Redress of Grievances* (New Haven: Yale University Press, 2012), 128–135, discussing the initiative and referendum process in the United States as a modern form of the classic right of petition.

also a means of mass communication that can be and is used by government and corporate interests to move public opinion in ways congenial to those holding the reins of government and corporate power. Because the same anonymity that empowers someone who has been victimized by sexualized violence also empowers the NRA and the Tobacco Institute, we need to be clear eyed in assessing the net social costs and benefits of privacy on the web. It is certainly true, as Professor Tushnet argues, that anonymity or the use of a pseudonym can be "positive"[82] and "defensive,"[83] but these devices also can be corrosive and distortionary.

Different national systems tolerate greater – or lesser – forms of anonymous or pseudonymous speech. Consideration of how other societies, sharing a common commitment to both the freedom of speech and privacy, have regulated anonymous and pseudonymous speech could provide valuable insights into the relevant costs and benefits of leaving these practices entirely unregulated, at one extreme, and using positive law to prohibit them completely, at the other. I do not take a firm position on whether either of these polar solutions would constitute the best potential policy, but it would be useful to see whether restrictions on such forms of speech do in fact produce significant, or only relatively minimal, chilling effects on an individual citizen's expressive activity.

[82] Tushnet, "The Yes Men ...," 122–123.
[83] *Ibid.*

Conclusion: embracing the possibilities of comparative law in the context of privacy

In conclusion, I would like to add a proposed "fifth" privacy myth to Professor Richards' excellent working list of privacy myths – to recap, "privacy is dead," "people don't care about privacy," "people with nothing to hide have nothing to fear," and "privacy is bad for business."[84] The fifth privacy myth is that privacy is such a culturally situated concept that transnational discussions of this subject are useless and bound to fail.

Professor James Whitman has written extensively and lucidly on the differences between US and European, particularly French and German, understandings of personal privacy. He concludes, based on his survey of the salient differences and underlying values, that privacy as a concept is not a particularly promising subject for transnational study and investigation. Because the scope and meaning of privacy vary so radically from place to place, and reflect deeply seated historical, social, cultural, and legal contingencies that are locally situated, it is very difficult to make meaningful – or useful – comparisons between legal systems regarding the proper scope and application of the concept.

Accordingly, Whitman strongly cautions against attempting to engage privacy (or dignity) across legal systems and

---

[84] See Richards, "Four Privacy Myths," 33–36.

cultures; in his view, doing so will not add much value.[85] Thus, he argues that "the emphases and sensibilities of the law on either side of the Atlantic remain stubbornly different, whatever careful philosophical logic might allow or dictate."[86] Professor Whitman's cautionary notes are certainly valid, and ought to give a reasonable person pause. Yet, there remains a clear and obvious transcultural salience to "privacy" that simply cannot be denied.[87] What is more, and as the preceding chapters clearly demonstrate, domestic discussions of privacy could clearly benefit from consideration of legal rules and cultural practices in democratic polities that share our commitment to safeguarding fundamental human rights.

I do not suggest that we could ever reach general agreement across national boundaries regarding the proper scope and meaning of privacy; to this extent, I will happily concede the validity of Professor Whitman's objections to the potential prospects for developing a comprehensive global law of privacy.[88] Congruence across and between legal systems with radically different baselines cannot and will not happen – French privacy norms are not Canadian privacy norms, and US privacy norms are different still. As Whitman

---

[85] Whitman, "The Two Western Cultures," 1219–1221.

[86] *Ibid.*, 1219.

[87] But cf. *ibid.*, 1221, "Of course, we are free to plead for a different kind of law in Europe or in the United States. But pleading for privacy as such is not the way to do it."

[88] See *ibid.*, 1219–1221.

suggests, "[w]e can opt for a world in which societies just do things differently."[89]

However, to say that convergence isn't a realistic goal is not to say that consideration of how other nations define and protect privacy rights is necessarily useless or unhelpful; even if we would never agree to import, lock, stock, and barrel another nation's privacy law, this does not mean that we could not potentially benefit from at least considering whether foreign polities have built a better mousetrap. To provide a concrete example, some European countries, and the European Court of Human Rights, embrace the concept of being private in public;[90] this doctrine has profound implications for the scope of protected free speech and free press

---

[89] *Ibid.*, 1221.

[90] See Bundesverfassungsgericht [BVerfG] [Federal Constitutional Court] (December 15, 1999), 101 Entcheidungen des Bundesverfassungsgerichts [BVERFGE] 361 (Ger.) ("Princess Caroline"), finding that the publication of some contested photos of the Princess would violate her privacy rights under the German constitution, notwithstanding the fact that the photographs were all taken in public places, but refusing to enjoin the publication of others; this decision was overruled in part by Von Hannover v. Germany, App. No. 59320/00, 40 Eur. H.R. Rep. 1 (2005), holding that the German court's ruling was insufficiently protective of the Princess's privacy rights under Article 8 of the European Convention and requiring an injunction against publication of most of the photographs at issue. Under the aegis of the tort of breach of confidence, the courts of the United Kingdom also have embraced the legal principle that it is possible to retain a reasonable expectation of privacy while in public. See Campbell v. MGN Ltd., [2004] UKHL 22, [2004] 2 A.C. (H.L.) 457 (appeal taken from England).

rights. I would never assert that the United States or Canada should reflexively import this doctrine into our domestic law; but we could benefit from at least considering the possibility that a person's mere presence on a street or sidewalk does not automatically defeat any claim of privacy.

Another example: whether it should be legally possible to alienate permanently and irrevocably one's privacy rights, at least with respect to one's personal image and identity. Whitman reports that French law makes certain privacy interests alienable contingently and thus only to a limited extent;[91] certain kinds of personal information and images may be reclaimed (even if previously sold).[92] The notion of only contingent, or limited, alienability of certain kinds of privacy interests might be tremendously useful in thinking about the problem of revenge porn[93] – if a significant other provides compromising photographs, the subject might be thought to retain the ability to, as it were, recall the photograph and prohibit its further distribution or publication. The permission to possess and distribute material of this sort might be thought both contingent and revocable. Nor would adopting this approach, at least in this context, do meaningful damage to core free speech and free press values.

In sum, I have made a sustained, and perhaps unduly detailed, argument that our domestic discussions of privacy

[91] Whitman, "The Two Western Cultures," 1174–1180.

[92] *Ibid.*, 1177–1178.

[93] Danielle Keats Citron & Mary Anne Franks, "Criminalizing Revenge Porn," *Wake Forest Law Review* 49 (2014).

could be improved and enhanced if we were to take into account how other nations, sharing common commitments to the rule of law, fundamental rights, and democratic self-government have defined the precise metes and bounds of privacy. This is not because foreign law is invariably better than our contemporary domestic law, but rather because consideration and awareness of different approaches to common problems will help us to better ascertain and understand the implicit costs and benefits of our existing legal and policy solutions.

At the end of the day, we might well conclude that the status quo ante represents the best possible policy – in light of our local legal, cultural, and philosophical understandings and traditions. But the exercise will surely result in a clearer appreciation of how our system succeeds – and fails – in safeguarding effectively "the right to be let alone."

Index

Index

Index

Index